MY
THE WISEGUYS

A Memoir

Carl Bilancione
with Troy Soos

Cobino Publishing

Table of Contents

1. Family Secrets

William Faulkner had it right: "The past is never dead. It's not even past." That's certainly been true of my family's history and the way it keeps intruding into my life. Of course, Faulkner didn't have a family like mine in mind when he wrote those words. Come to think of it, maybe the guy I should be quoting is Michael Corleone: "Just when I thought I was out, they pull me back in!"

I left Brooklyn more than fifty years ago and put many of the memories of those days behind me. During that time, I'd built a very different life for myself from the one I'd grown up in, with a number of achievements and an exciting year coming up.

In a few months I would be retiring from a successful dental practice, giving me more time to spend with my wife Deborah. I planned to resume the sports talk shows that I'd hosted a few years earlier, a publisher was pressing me to do a book of my wildlife photography, I was being recruited for another reality television series and I'd been asked to speak at the world premiere of Burt Reynolds' final film in which I'd had a small role. Yet, with so much to look forward to, one phone call suddenly had me looking backward.

***

In March 2022, I'm sitting on the patio of my lake-front home in Florida on a clear Saturday night, just relaxing and looking at the lights reflected on the water. At nine o'clock my phone rings. It's my cousin Leo from upstate New York and he's not relaxed at all. In fact, he's in a panic.

"You're not gonna believe this," he says. "I got a sister!"

"I know, you got two of them: Donna and Francesca." How could he think this was news?

"No, I mean *another* one. Her name's Elizabeth—she goes by 'Lizzie'—and she's my half-sister."

"How do you know that?"

"This Lizzie just called me out of the blue. She says she and her best friend growing up in Brooklyn always wondered who they might be related to—her friend was adopted, so who knows, right? Anyway, they both took those DNA tests that can tell you about your ancestry. And can you believe it? Lizzie and me have the same father!" Leo was so agitated, he had to pause for breath before continuing. "I quizzed her to see if it could be true, and her answers all fit. Besides, DNA doesn't lie. My pop had an illegitimate kid and she's my sister!"

Considering some of the other things my Uncle Sal had been involved with, learning that he'd been unfaithful to his wife wasn't the biggest shock I'd ever had. "What did she sound like?" I asked. "Was she nice?"

"Yeah, I guess she was. But why is she getting in touch with me? Does she want something from me? Money? I'm not giving her no money!"

"Maybe she just wants to make a connection," I suggested. "She discovered she has family she didn't know about and she's curious. That's understandable."

Leo grunted. "I hope you feel the same way about yours."

"Mine?"

"Yeah. That friend of hers who also got tested... turns out she's *your* sister. And she wants to give you a call."

Now I *was* shocked. A dozen questions immediately came to mind but the only one I could think to ask was, "What's her name?"

"Susan."

"Give her my number," I said.

***

I had only a few minutes to try to absorb the impact of the news before my phone rang.

When I answered, a soft, pleasant voice said hesitatingly, "Hi Carl, this is Susan."

"Hey Sis, how you doing?" She laughed at my greeting. "So you're my half-sister," I said. "I guess we should talk."

She agreed, and explained how the relationships were discovered. Susan and Lizzie had grown up in the old neighborhood a few houses apart. They were inseparable friends and remained close through the years. The biggest surprise to them from their DNA results wasn't the identities of their biological fathers, but the fact that they were actually related to each other. Lizzie had the bloodline of my Uncle Sal, and Susan had my father's, so that made them cousins.

"That must have been quite a surprise," I said. "And the DNA test is how you found out about my family, too?"

"No, I knew my background all along." According to Susan, her birth-mother had told her that she'd resulted from a single encounter with Carlo Bilancione at a motel in Sheepshead Bay. When he found out that he'd gotten the woman pregnant, my father forced her to give the baby up for adoption to a local couple who hadn't been able to have children of their own. "They were the most wonderful, loving people," Susan stressed. "They were my *parents*, my 'father' and my 'mother,' and I won't use those words for the woman who gave birth to me or for your father."

"You've known this all along, and this is the first time you're getting in touch with us?" Why now? I wondered. Why wait all these years?

"No, I contacted your father about thirty years ago—and that did not go well."

"In person?"

"No, I called him."

That was a relief to hear—he couldn't have hit her over the phone. My father had three basic response settings: surly, hostile and violent. People who caught him in a surly mood were the lucky ones. "What did he say?"

Susan struggled for a moment to go on, but I sensed it was more because of discomfort at the memory of the conversation than any reluctance to relate it to me. "Well, the first thing he said to me was, 'You're not my daughter.' I started to give him details, then he suddenly demanded, 'What do you look like?' I assumed he wanted to know if there was a physical resemblance that would help convince him. But after I described myself, he said, 'You sound pretty hot, just like your mother. You know, when I saw her ass walking to the bus stop I said to myself *I gotta get her in bed*. And I did, but just the one time, no big deal. Your mother was nothing but a hit-and-run for me, that's all she was.' I was appalled, totally speechless. I couldn't believe any man could be so rude. I hung up the phone and vowed never to contact him again."

For a minute I couldn't respond to Susan's story. I was furious that my father would speak that way to the woman who'd resulted from his 'hit-and-run' and disgusted that he would term it that way. I tried to stammer an apology for her experience but couldn't find the words. "I don't have any contact with him anymore, either," I finally said. "I try not to be like him."

"According to what I've read, you're not."

"What have you been reading?"

"Well, that's kind of a funny story. In 2002, my birth-mother called me and told me to take a look at the *New York Times*. She said there was an article in there that I might like to read. That's when I learned that your father was in the... you know."

Yes, I did know. I'd had a growing suspicion over the years but didn't *know* until I'd read the new reports: My father, Carlo Bilancione, whom I used to think was simply a hard-working longshoreman, was identified as part of the Genovese crime family. He'd been arrested in a crackdown on mob influence at the New Jersey docks. Around the same time that I was heading to Kenya for my stint on *Survivor Africa*, my father was heading to New Jersey State Prison in Trenton.

Susan continued, "What was funny is that, when I searched online for more news about your father, the name *Carl* Bilancione kept coming up. I did a little more digging and learned that you're Carlo's son—my brother. Over the years, I'd look up a little more about you and check your social media now and then. You've done some impressive things—you're a dentist, you've been on television shows, you do charitable work for children. I have to say, you don't seem anything like your father."

"I hope not," I replied. "There's something I don't understand, though: You've known about me for twenty years and never tried to make contact before. Why not?"

"Well, I've had a very happy life, with kind, loving parents. And now a wonderful husband and beautiful children of my own." She hesitated. "I have the feeling your childhood wasn't quite so happy and I wasn't sure if you'd want to talk to somebody who'd remind you of those days."

Actually, I did want to. Very much.

The phone call lasted until three in the morning and the conversation was as comfortable as it was enlightening. Where we grew up, everybody somehow "knew" everything without anything being explicitly expressed in words. *You don't talk* was a commandment more strictly observed than any laws. But the two of us talked freely this evening. Having grown up in the same neighborhood as me, she knew things that I didn't and I was able to fill in some blanks for her.

Susan and I spoke often after that first call, readily sharing our histories. And some questions that had puzzled me all my life began to have answers.

2. Brooklyn

If my father hadn't been arrested for breaking into cars on Coney Island, I would never have been born. That arrest wouldn't be his last, nor his most notorious, but it was significant to me because it resulted in him meeting my mother.

At sixteen years old, my father, together with a group of fellow drop-outs, got busted and had to face a judge for the first time. The judge made him an offer he couldn't refuse: jail or the military. The United States Navy thus acquired the services of seaman recruit Carlo Bilancione.

He was initially stationed at Guantanamo Bay, where he got involved in some misadventures, and was then shipped north to Naval Station Argentia in Newfoundland. That's where he met his future wife who was working at the base's Navy Exchange.

Vivian May Hollett, two years older than my father, was a pretty, petite woman with auburn hair and beautiful blue eyes. She came from Adam's Cove, a little fishing village on the coast of Conception Bay in Newfoundland. The men of Adam's Cove were fishermen or worked in the nearby mines and lumber camps. Her father was a miner who died of cancer at age thirty-one, leaving a widow and five girls to fend for themselves. My mother had to drop out of school after the ninth grade to help support the family and felt fortunate to get a job at the naval base. Like my father, she came from poor, working-class people and didn't have much formal education.

The six Hollett women were a tight-knit family, very religious with strict morals and traditional beliefs. They struggled to survive, but were always determined to maintain their values and lead decent lives. The Bilanciones, in contrast, were male-dominated and as far as decency... Well, they lived by a code of their own.

Whatever differences there might have been in their characters, a romance developed and my father proposed. This made my mother happy and my grandfather furious—my mother wasn't American and, worse than that, not Italian. Although he initially tried to forbid the marriage, my parents went ahead and had a naval wedding in the Argentia chapel.

I was born in Chelsea Naval Hospital near Boston in June 1955, nine months to the day after they were wed. Since my father still had six months to go in the Navy, my mother and I remained in Massachusetts living with her sister Dorothy.

After my father's discharge, the three of us moved to Brooklyn where we would reside on the middle floor of my grandfather's house in the southern part of the borough. When my father introduced my mother to his family, they spat at her and called her a "whore." It was an awful way for my mother to discover that she had joined a very different family from the one she'd left in Newfoundland.

***

My grandfather had been born in Naples. At a time when many Italians came to America for a better life, my grandfather came because of a more pressing need: While still in his teens he had killed a man and needed to flee the country. I can't prove he committed that crime, but it was the story everyone in the family knew and didn't doubt. Since my grandfather lacked the fare for passage, he got a job as a deck hand on the *Castel Porziano* and jumped ship when it reached New York. On June 15, 1922, Armondo Bilancione passed through Ellis Island, safely beyond the reach of the Italian authorities.

He first lived in Hell's Kitchen on Manhattan's west side, where he found a job on the docks. He met Anna Mazza, also from Naples, whom he married in 1923 and they began a family that would total nine children. Hell's Kitchen was a rough place to live in those days. The housing was mostly tenements and the streets were ruled by gangs. As soon as they could, they moved to Brooklyn where the houses were nicer and the crime was better organized.

We never knew how my grandfather could afford to buy a three-story house in Brooklyn so soon after arriving penniless in the country, and we never wanted to ask him about it. He was a mean, violent man who always carried a knife and pulled it readily. Even without the knife, he was dangerous, short in stature but made of solid muscle and willing to take on anybody in a fight. He was also quick to discipline his children. If any of his kids got out of line, he tied them to a pipe in the basement and beat them mercilessly. It's no surprise that most of his sons turned out to be violent too.

My Uncle Vito was the worst. He was a Golden Gloves boxer who probably could have won a championship. But he got involved with the mob, took a dive, and that was the end of his boxing career. He became a fruit peddler, riding his little truck around the neighborhood. Since he couldn't throw punches in the ring anymore, he directed them at easier targets. He beat his kids so badly that my cousin Elaine didn't have a tooth left in her mouth. He later killed a woman with his bare fist, but no one could prove it.

The closest of my grandfather's sons were my father Carlo and my uncle Sal, who had a lot in common. They were both born in 1935, my father early in the year and my uncle at the end, and they both worked as longshoremen, getting their jobs through my grandfather who had an influential position in the union. And they were both *tough*. My dad was usually called "Rocky" or "Rock." He was only about five-nine and a hundred fifty pounds, but his muscles were indeed rock-hard. People said he could throw a punch that would make you see stars. I can attest to that because there were a couple of times when I got to view entire galaxies. Uncle Sal, short and stocky, was called "Sal the Bull" to distinguish him from the hundred other "Sal"s in the neighborhood as well as from a certain Sammy the Bull who was starting his career not far from us in Bensonhurst.

***

Not only were the Bilanciones a very different family from the one my mother had left behind, but the environment was a drastic change as well. Adam's Cove had only a hundred or so inhabitants when my mother lived there. Years later, it combined with several other small communities to raise its status from "village" to "town." It was a scenic spot, with waves breaking on its rocky coast, and a landscape of forests and mountains.

Brooklyn was crowded with more than two million inhabitants. And of course there were no mountains or forests, although the brick and the concrete could rise pretty high. We lived on Bay 47th Street and the closest beach was Bath Beach. However, the "beach" was now asphalt instead of sand, having been paved over for the Shore Parkway before I was born.

Our neighborhood was predominantly Italian, together with a sizable Jewish population and a few Irish. Those groups all got along fairly well together. Blacks lived in the Marlboro housing projects not far from Lafayette High School. For the most part, we stayed clear of them and they stayed clear of us. As long as territorial boundaries were respected, there was little conflict.

There was crime in the area but not much of what you'd call street crime. A woman could walk to the store or go to evening Mass without fear of being mugged. The local wiseguys wouldn't stand for anything like that. In the 1950s and 60s, the Mob was at the height of its power and determined a lot of what went on in the city. They preferred to keep the violent crime between themselves as the different families and factions vied for dominance. I don't know how many times I saw cars on Bath Avenue with police tape around them; a body was often found in the trunk, or the car had been firebombed.

A lot of extra-legal activities were tolerated—and generally appreciated—by the local residents. No one had any trouble finding a place to lay down a bet, get into a card or craps game, buy tax-free cigarettes or take out a short-term loan. And almost any kind of goods could be bought at a heavy discount—enough merchandise "fell off the back of a truck" to stock both Macy's and Gimbels.

Basically, we lived the real version of what was later fictionalized in the movie *Goodfellas*. There was even a bar called The Hole in the Wall, similar to the Bamboo Lounge in the movie, where the wiseguys hung out. My father and Uncle Sal used to frequent the place.

***

We lived in my grandfather's house for the first twelve years of my life, but we were never really welcome. My parents rented a two-bedroom apartment on the second floor, and we were prohibited from going onto any other part of the property. I don't think the restriction bothered my parents much, but it didn't provide much room for us kids to play.

There was a spacious backyard, but we weren't allowed to step foot in it. The garage was off-limits too. One Christmas, my father bought nice new bikes for my brother and me, probably from one of those "back of the truck" sales. We loved those bikes and pleaded with my grandfather to let us keep them in the garage. He refused, and said we had to keep them outside. Even though we chained them to a fence, they were gone the next morning.

We were occasionally invited into the basement for family gatherings. This basement was infamous as the place where my father and his siblings were disciplined and famous for the bootleg wine my grandfather used to manufacture there. He operated on such a scale that he was once raided by the Alcohol Tax Unit of the Bureau of Internal Revenue, predecessor to the ATF. Thanks to a tip, though, he had the basement clean and everything hidden by the time the agents arrived.

Those infrequent visits to the basement were my favorite memories of my grandfather. His wine-making days over, it was the place where he prepared holiday meals. He was an excellent cook and introduced me to dishes I still love to eat: stuffed zucchini blossoms, parmigiana di melanzane, pasta fagioli e cozze and snails in red sauce. Even at those family events, though, we were treated as outsiders because we weren't fully Italian.

Two years after I was born, my brother Anthony came along and I had a playmate. Anthony was a cheerful, chubby kid who liked to clown around. There was a bond between us, right from the start and we did everything together growing up.

Since we couldn't play in the yard, the street became our playground. Like most kids in Brooklyn we played stoop ball, punch ball and of course stickball with those pink rubber balls. We were poor, so we couldn't afford the preferred Spaldeen balls and had to use the cheaper Pensie Pinkie brand. The Spaldeens were twelve cents and the Pensie Pinkies only cost a dime. When the ball began to lose its bounce, my mother would put it in boiling water to restore it; that way we could go a while longer before we'd have to scrape up enough pennies for a new one. We had to save every cent in those days.

The other great fun we had on the street was during the festivals. The Catholic church near us, Most Precious Blood Church, would hold a week-long street festival every summer. For kids, there were games like the milk bottle ring toss and a goldfish bowl where you'd throw a ping pong ball into the bowl to try to win one of the fish. The adults liked to try for prizes of Lucky Strike cigarettes. There was great street food—I was especially fond of the zeppolas with powdered sugar. Everybody would be out on the street having a good time, talking to their neighbors, laughing, playing games. It was a great way for the community to be together.

After Anthony, my sister Debbie was born, but she only lived six months. Her loss completely devastated my mother. Then I had two more brothers and a sister. As the oldest child in the family, I now had to start doing my part to help out.

***

My father left for his job at the docks early every morning without knowing if he would be hired. In those days, longshoremen had to show up for what they called the "shape-up." The hiring boss would look over the crowd of hopefuls and point to the ones who were going to get work that day. Kickbacks to the boss could help guide his selections. Some of the longshoremen would signal to him the amount they were willing to kick back, almost like a bidding war. My father was only in his twenties and still low man on the totem pole. It would be years before he would rise to a position in the union from which he could be on the receiving end of those offers. So his income was uncertain and we remained poor.

Whether my father got work or not, he'd be gone for the day and never said where. That left my mother to manage things at home, which was quite a challenge. My father never allowed her to get a job or drive a car, and she was supposed to cook for him at whatever time he showed up, keep the apartment clean, produce children and raise them. Before I was in kindergarten, I started helping my mother with her responsibilities.

Even if she had been allowed to drive, it would have been difficult for my mother to leave the house since she had to stay with the younger children. None of our relatives would ever watch them for her, not even in an emergency. If something needed to be done outside the house, it fell to me.

We didn't have a washer or dryer, so every Saturday I took care of the wash, lugging it to a laundry down the street along with my schoolwork or a book to read. I'd study until the laundry was finished, then bring it all back home for my mother to iron.

I also did the grocery shopping. My mother gave me money and a list specifying exactly what I should get and which brand. She always picked the ones she thought would be cheapest since we had to stretch every dollar. Once I started school, I turned out to have a knack for math and began to choose the brands myself. At first my mother was upset that I'd gotten the wrong ones and had squandered our money. But I showed her how I'd calculated the cost per ounce for each can and actually got the best deals. It was my little contribution to the family finances.

Every Sunday, I walked with Anthony to Fisherman's Methodist Church on Cropsey Avenue. My father dictated almost everything for our family, but there were a few issues on which my mother prevailed. She was devoutly religious, raised Methodist, and wanted her children brought up in the same faith. Although he'd been an alter boy, and the Bilanciones were nominally Catholic, my father never tried to get my mother to convert and he let us go to the Methodist church.

My mother was always grateful for my help and would try to do special things for me in return. When I wanted to go fishing, she bundled all of the kids together and walked us almost two miles to the Verrazzano bridge for me to try it. I had the most wonderful time, and only wished I could have caught something that we could have put on the dinner plates.

***

In another concession to my mother, my father drove us all to Massachusetts once a year in order for her to see her sister in Revere. She's the one we had lived with while my father finished out his navy enlistment. Aunt Dot and Uncle Eric were the nicest people on earth, warm and welcoming, totally different from my Brooklyn relatives. It was here that I began to experience the freedom of the outdoors. I walked along the canals, fished and rode my bike. Nearby in Malden is where I learned to swim. Compared to the city streets I was used to, Revere was Aruba.

Another place I looked forward to visiting was Grahamsville, New York, where Uncle Sal owned a cabin. Every now and then, my father would get the itch to get out of the city and drive us up. Talk about rural! This place was on the side of a mountain in the Catskills, near Rondout Reservoir. I was let loose to roam wherever I wanted, and I wandered all over those woods trying to catch snakes and frogs and looking for birds and squirrels.

I developed an appreciation of nature and wildlife during these outings that has remained with me. Later, it inspired me to visit other parts of the world where I got to see creatures and scenery that I couldn't even imagine in Brooklyn.

***

I started elementary school at PS 212, a huge brick building on Bay 49th Street. From the beginning, I was a conscientious student and always got good grades.

One reason I did well in school is that I had a vivid imagination and a natural curiosity—I *wanted* to learn. Another was that I didn't want to get smacked. I figured if I made good grades, at least I'd never get hit because of a bad report card. Homework and studying were a priority for me, along with helping my mother. When we finally got a television set in our home, it was never turned on until I'd finished my schoolwork. Even then, we weren't allowed to watch much of it, only a few family shows like *Mutual of*

Omaha's Wild Kingdom and *Walt Disney's Wonderful World of Color* which we viewed in flickering black-and-white.

I successfully avoided getting into trouble because of academics, but I made one blunder that almost landed me in the hospital. When I was in kindergarten, a girl came up and kissed me. In response, I hit her on the shoulder. I shouldn't have, but I was a five-year-old boy who simply didn't want some icky girl kissing me. Well, the girl's father showed up at our door that night. He told my dad, "Your son hit my daughter."

"Which son?" He dragged Anthony and me to the door. The girl's dad pointed to me, and my father began to beat the living daylights out of me. He was called "Rocky" even before he was a longshoreman; now, after years of lifting crates his muscles were like steel cables.

I was getting it so bad that the girl's father tried to intervene. My father told him, "I'll take care of *my* kids *my* way," and threw him out. Then he turned his attention back to me and went a few more rounds with me as a punching bag.

I was five years old and had already known for a long time that there had to be a better way to live. Somehow, I had to break free from the kind of life in which I was growing up.

***

At first, I only considered what I *didn't* want: I didn't want to live with violence, I didn't want to work the same kinds of jobs as my father and uncles, and I didn't want to be confined to one street in Brooklyn.

Eventually, I discovered what I did want: I wanted to be a baseball player. Baseball was my first love. I read about the players and collected every card. I wasn't allowed to watch the games on television, though, because my father hated sports—unless you count poker as a sport. He never taught us to play baseball or football, and we never attended any games.

When I was nine years old, my Uncle Lloyd took me to Yankee Stadium. This was the first and only big-league game I went to while we lived in Brooklyn. When I walked into that magnificent ballpark I was in total awe. This was 1964, Yogi Berra was managing, and the Yankees were on their way to another pennant. They still had some of their great players—Mickey Mantle, Roger Maris, Whitey Ford, Elston Howard. I must have been the most excited kid in the stadium when Mantle hit a home run to win the game!

When I came home, I informed my mother that I wanted to be a baseball player. She'd always supported me and encouraged me in everything I did, and this time was no different. She promptly signed me up to play ball in the Police Athletic League. Never mind that wanting to be a baseball player and having the ability to play ball were two different things. My mother believed I could do anything I set my mind to.

I got on my bike and rode to the baseball field, peddling extra fast when I passed by the projects since that turf was off-limits to kids from my neighborhood. At the park, I was given a uniform and was thrilled to see number 7 on the back of my jersey. I had the same number as Mickey

Mantle! Surely that was an omen that I'd made the right career choice.

The coach asked me what position I played. I had never played any position but thought pitcher would be a good one. He let me try, but I stumbled trying to pitch from a mound. There are no mounds in stickball and I'd never been taught how to throw from one. I was next sent to center field. That made sense to me because Mantle was a centerfielder and we did have the same uniform number. Wouldn't you know, in my first game I hit a home run and biked home convinced I was going on to the big leagues!

When I got to the house, I found my father was home earlier than usual. He looked at me in my uniform and asked my mother, "What the hell is he wearing?"

She told him she'd signed me up for the PAL baseball team, and assured him that it hadn't cost anything and wouldn't interfere with my chores or my schoolwork.

The next day I had to turn in my uniform. My father said I wasn't a good enough fighter to go near the projects. I had to quit the team.

**

My short-lived baseball fantasy over, I began to work even harder at school. Education, I'd concluded, was going to be my way out.

Here, too, my mother gave me the most support and encouragement. Despite her own limited education, she often sat up with me to help me in my studies. She liked to remind me what my kindergarten teacher, Mrs. Bell, had said to her at a parent conference years earlier: "Carl is my favorite student. He is so bright and energetic, he's sure to be a big success. Someday he could be the first man on the moon." My mother was in complete agreement with Mrs. Bell.

The truth is, despite all the tough guys around me, who relied on muscles and violence, the strongest person in my life was my mother. She accepted her living situation without complaint, did everything she could for her children and instilled in me the courage to believe in myself.

At night, after my schoolwork was finished, I continued to learn by reading books. I had a little nightlight next to my bed so that I could read without disturbing my brother. I especially liked to read biographies and autobiographies of successful people like Andrew Carnegie and the Rockefellers. But the book that made the strongest impression was Walt Disney's autobiography.

Disney said, "If you can dream it, you can do it." I adopted it as my motto and hoped that it was true. Because I was beginning to have some pretty big dreams.

3. A Nerd at Newfield

I don't think anyone was ever happier about being evicted than I was when my grandfather threw us out. My Aunt Carmela had decided that she wanted our apartment for her own family. Since she was my grandfather's favorite child, despite having committed the egregious offence of marrying a non-Italian, she got her wish and we needed to find a new home.

My parents had to look far from the city to find a house that we could afford, which was fine by me. They settled on a narrow, one-story home on a tiny lot in Selden, Long Island. The house cost $12,900—this was in 1967—and they were concerned about paying so much.

The place wasn't spacious but it suited our needs. The four boys shared a bedroom with double bunk beds and a single dresser. As the two oldest, Anthony and I got the top bunks. I immediately installed my nightlight on the headboard and a bookshelf next to it so that I could continue my habit of reading into the night.

The area was rural in those days; there were a few other houses nearby, but not enough to call it a neighborhood. There were no sidewalks, and our backyard was bordered by woods that had a large population of squirrels. My father liked to shoot at them from a bedroom window and no one ever complained.

There were some inconveniences to living in a place so remote. Until I was sixteen and could get a driver's license, I still had to walk to do the grocery shopping for my mother.

That wasn't much of an excursion in Brooklyn, but the nearest store to our new home was Aggie's Deli about a mile away. At least we had a washing machine now, so I no longer had to lug our clothes back-and-forth to a laundromat.

The move to Selden meant that my father had a long commute. He worked on the docks in Bayonne, New Jersey, a two-hour drive each way. He left the house at four every morning, and of course my mother was up before that in order to make him breakfast. He liked to tell us what a sacrifice he was making to give us a better life away from the city. Later, I learned that he preferred to keep his home life well-distanced from his other activities.

When we moved to Long Island, I was due to enter the seventh grade. The school had different academic levels and I was given an assessment to determine where I should be placed. Unfortunately, I'm one of those students who sometimes struggles on standardized tests. I did so badly on this exam, that I was labeled mentally challenged and assigned to a remedial class. I was only in it for a few hours before my teacher realized that I'd been misplaced. She sent me to a guidance counselor and I was reassigned to academic classes. Two weeks after that, I was again summoned to the guidance office and promoted to the honors level.

Throughout junior high school, I remained committed to my studies, never doubting that education was my ticket to success. For some time, I'd had a vague notion of becoming a pilot. I had always liked to look up and see the planes overhead as they flew to and from JFK and LaGuardia airports. Perhaps the attraction was that I was seeking an escape and could imagine no better one than soaring above the clouds. By the time I entered high school, although I knew no more about flying a plane than I did about pitching from a mound, I was pretty sure I would become an airline pilot.

**

It was a rite of passage among the Bilanciones that when a boy turned fourteen he would be taken hunting. Every year, the week before Thanksgiving, my father and uncles, together with a few friends, would go deer hunting. A butcher they knew processed their kills and the venison was distributed throughout the family for holiday meals.

When I reached the age to be invited on this annual hunt, I completed the required safety courses and traveled with my father and uncle to the rustic cabin in Grahamsville. I was excited to go, partly because I felt that I was being accepted as a man, but primarily because one of the other guests was an airline pilot. I wanted to learn everything I could from him.

As far as the actual hunting, I had no desire to kill an animal and was determined that I wouldn't do so. On the first day of the hunt, I was dressed head-to-toe in orange and positioned near an apple orchard. The adults would drive any deer toward me, making it easy for me to bag my first one. A buck eventually came into the orchard, and I just watched it feed, admiring its graceful movements. I raised my rifle, but only so that I could see the beautiful creature more clearly through the scope. The men finally came to me and asked why I didn't shoot. I lied and said I hadn't seen a thing. My father was furious.

The next day, my dad escorted me to the woods and remained nearby to keep an eye on me. It wasn't long before a six-point buck came into view. Fortunately for the animal, he made his appearance while my father was relieving himself. With his pants around his ankles, my father awkwardly tried to shoot but failed. I didn't fire at all, and claimed it was because I feared accidentally hitting my father. That was the closest either one of us came to getting a deer.

I spent more time in the cabin than in the woods on that trip, studying the schoolbooks I'd brought with me and getting up the courage to ask the pilot about his job. I'm rarely shy about talking to people, but I was hesitant to speak to this man. So far, he was a complete disappointment, nothing like what I'd expected of a pilot. He was an obnoxious slob who did little more than drink and look at the supply of porn he'd brought with him. Although my father and uncles didn't say anything to him about his conduct, I could tell that even they were disgusted—and they did not set a very high bar for acceptable social behavior.

I finally approached the man and told him I was thinking of becoming a pilot. Did he have any advice for me? I asked.

"Yeah," he slurred. "Don't be like me." He pointed an unsteady finger at one of the other friends of my uncle. "That's the guy you want to be like. Go talk to him." The pilot drank another slug of bourbon and turned his attention back to his porn.

The fellow he'd indicated was a well-dressed man of about forty with an easy-going manner. He had driven up to the cabin in a silver Mercedes convertible, which was not a vehicle I was accustomed to seeing. The man was a dentist, and apparently a successful one. I don't remember his name because everyone simply called him "Doc."

Up to this time, my experiences with dentists were not positive ones. Our family couldn't afford regular dentists, so we had to use a free clinic in Manhattan that was affiliated with the longshoremen's union. The staff there treated us like beggars.

This dentist, though, turned out to be a gentleman. He spoke to me about his profession and treated me with courtesy. He pointed out that there was job security in dentistry since people would always need dental work. And it was a profession that allowed you to really help people, whether by relieving their pain or by improving their appearance and making them feel better about themselves.

The more I considered it, the more certain I was that this was the career for me. By establishing my own practice, I could be my own boss and never have to be dependent on anyone else. Dentistry would allow me to earn a good living as well as care for other people.

The hunting trip was now a complete success: I had killed nothing and had settled on my future profession.

***

On the Monday after we returned from Grahamsville, I went directly to the office of Mr. Wallace, our guidance counselor at Newfield High School. He'd been at the school for years, patiently listened to students with all kind of problems and questions, and did his best to assist them. A student could tell him he wanted to become a rock star or an astronaut, and Mr. Wallace would consider the matter seriously and calmly advise the best path for achieving that goal.

I asked what I needed to do to become a dentist.

"Why a dentist?" he asked. "If you're interested in the medical field, why not become a doctor? You're always helping other kids with their school work. I know you'd have a great bedside manner with patients."

I explained that I didn't want to go into hospitals filled with sick people, deal with death or make house calls—which many doctors still did back then. I insisted that I wanted to be a dentist. In only a few days, I had developed tunnel vision: My sight was set on dentistry and I was determined to embark on the most direct path toward achieving my objective.

"Whether medical school or dental school," Mr. Wallace said, "that only comes after your undergraduate degree. You'll need to keep your grades up to get into a good college."

That would be no problem, I assured him. I knew that I could earn the grades.

"That means four years of college tuition." He cleared his throat. "Can your parents afford it?"

"Nope."

"Then you'll need to earn a scholarship. *Good* grades won't be enough. You'll need to make *top* grades."

I thanked Mr. Wallace, not at all discouraged. In fact, I was cheerful. He had told me what I needed to do, and I was confident that I had the ability to execute it.

I applied myself to my schoolwork so intently that my sisters and brothers derisively called me a "nerd," always with same snarling tone that was used for "rat" in the old neighborhood. I laughed it off; after all, it was pretty accurate. Besides, unlike a rat, no one had ever gotten whacked for being a nerd.

I was motivated and stable, and in truth was probably viewed as fairly boring. Despite it being the early '70s, I never tried drugs and didn't drink or smoke. If I had studying to do, I didn't care if you offered me tickets to see Elvis Presley—I was going to study. Giving anything less than my best effort would have been failure as far as I was concerned.

In addition to my own work, I helped other students as a volunteer tutor through the National Honor Society. I was voted president of the society three years in a row and enjoyed carrying out my responsibilities and working with others.

When report cards came out, we had to show them to my father. My brother Anthony didn't care much about school, his grades reflected it, and he was routinely grounded or given a smack for his performance. Unlike Anthony, I was proud of my grades; they were the payoff for all the struggles I'd put into earning them. When my father looked at my report card, he'd scowl and wordlessly stick it in his pocket. With every report card I handed him, I always hoped that he would give me at least a single word of praise. That notion remained a fantasy.

One night, my father came home at eleven o'clock and I was at the dining room table with several textbooks open in front of me. "What's he doing?" he asked my mother. Only in his thirties, his voice was already raspy from a four-pack-a-day cigarette habit.

She told him that I'd come home after track practice and had been studying ever since for a test the next day.

"He never has any friends over," my father groused. "Just his goddamn books."

Of course I didn't invite friends to the house. Why would I put them in jeopardy? My father was a violent man who used his fists without provocation, especially if he'd had a couple of Rheingolds too many.

"And why the hell isn't he out chasing girls?" As my father stared at me poring over my textbook, his expression hardened. "Sonofabitch!" he yelled. "You're gay!"

I just looked up at him, then back down at my book, trying not to smile.

***

In fact, I had a girlfriend and we were serious about each other.

I had met Bonnie Ann Behling in the ninth grade and we were instantly smitten with each other. She was a pretty girl, Italian-German, with dark hair and a lithe build. Our personalities were different—I was ambitious and seldom shy to speak my mind, while Bonnie was quiet and restrained—but we fit well together.

Bonnie was from a large family and had had a difficult childhood. Her parents divorced when she was young and Bonnie had lived with her mother in California. When her mother suddenly died of a heart attack, Bonnie had to move to Long Island to live with her father. He was remarried to a woman who had children of her own and resented the addition of a daughter from her husband's previous marriage. Bonnie's new mom modeled herself after the evil stepmother in *Cinderella*, and assigned her all the cleaning, laundry and any other menial jobs that came to mind.

When I introduced Bonnie to my family, they all hit it off right away. Even my father liked her. She was so easy-going and amiable that it was impossible not to get along with her. Bonnie enjoyed being with my family more than with her own, which is a good indicator of how rough her home life must have been.

There was one memorable conflict involving Bonnie, but it wasn't between the two of us. I wanted to take her to a school dance, but wasn't yet sixteen and couldn't drive. My father offered to drive us and I naively took him up on his offer. We hadn't even driven a mile before he started asking Bonnie the rudest and most embarrassing questions—almost as if he wanted her to confirm for him that I was not gay. I was seething, but didn't say anything in front of Bonnie.

After the dance, we dropped Bonnie off at her house and went home to ours. As soon as we were inside, my mother asked, "How did it go?"

"Horrible!" I yelled. Jerking my thumb at my father, I said, "He embarrassed me like you wouldn't believe. I'm never going *anywhere* with him again!"

My father went ballistic. "What? I'm an *embarrassment* to you?" He threw me against the living room wall. Using one of his favorite moves, he grabbed my throat with his left hand and pinned me to the wall. His right hand balled into a fist.

Terrified, my five-foot-two mother tried to squeeze between us, but my father pushed her aside.

He was about to unleash the punch when I said, "Go ahead." Barely able to squeeze out the words because of his vise-like grip, I went on, "You hit me now, I'm leaving and you'll never see me again." I had no reason to believe my words would have any effect; I was just a teenaged boy who'd been embarrassed in front of his girlfriend and was lashing out in anger.

My father hesitated in surprise, then lowered his fist and let go of my throat. It was the first time he had ever backed down and the last time that he put his hands on me.

***

Starting in the tenth grade, I ran track and cross country at Newfield. All those miles of walking that I did over the years doing errands for my mother had given me strong legs and I usually finished near the front of the pack.

Since I was fast, and almost six foot tall with a solid build, the school's football coach tried to recruit me. He thought I might make a good wide receiver. I turned him down. "I don't like getting hit," I told him. "And I don't want to hit anyone else." I'd had plenty of negative experiences with hitting, and contact sports held no appeal for me.

Bonnie was an excellent athlete, playing softball and volleyball, so athletics was another thing we had in common. But my desire to spend time with her cost me my running career—and a potential scholarship.

Our track coach was George Rhea, who had coached at the Olympic training center in Colorado Springs. He took running seriously and expected us to make it our number one priority too. That's asking a lot of hormone-fueled teenaged boys.

Two weeks before a big state meet, we were ordered to complete a ten-mile practice run. That's long in both distance and duration—an hour and a half minimum, closer to two. A couple of the senior boys also had girlfriends and it occurred to us that there was a more enjoyable way to spend that time. We started out with the group, then each ran off our separate ways. I went to see Bonnie for a while and returned to school about the time I figured the ten miles would be completed. The two seniors arrived shortly after me.

Coach Rhea summoned us to his office. "How was the run?" he asked.

We all said it was great.

"You're a bunch of liars!" he stormed. "You went to see your girlfriends! If you want to spend time with them instead of the team, you got it: All three of you are done for the season."

I was humiliated and it was my own fault. Then, stupidly, I made the situation even worse.

When the next season's first practice took place, I didn't go. Coach Rhea came to me the next day at lunch and asked, "Where the hell were you yesterday?"

"You kicked me off the team."

"That was last season. I want you to run for us again."

I stubbornly refused, and it turned out to cost me some badly needed scholarship money. I didn't know it at the time, but our school named a graduating senior as "scholar-athlete" each year, a title that came with a small scholarship. It was awarded to the varsity athlete with the highest grade point average. Had I continued with the team, I was a cinch to get the award since my grades were at the top of the class.

***

Teachers can have an enormous impact on their students. One word of encouragement can make their spirits soar; one harsh criticism can dash their hopes. I was fortunate that most of my teachers were encouragers.

In my junior year, though, I had an honors English teacher named Mr. Gehring. He always wore a short-sleeved white shirt with a striped tie, and horn-rimmed glasses that were perpetually on the verge of sliding off the end of his nose. He knew his subject, and taught it well, but he made it clear that he considered himself a superior being to us students.

I don't know why it came up in an English class, but one day Mr. Gehring went around the room and asked each student what car they hoped to own someday. Most of the students picked sports cars, everything from Corvettes to Ferraris.

When my turn came, I recalled the car that I had seen Doc driving at the hunting cabin. "A Mercedes," I answered. The choice wasn't because I had an ambition to own an expensive German car. I chose it because I was going to be a dentist and had gotten it into my head that that was the car a dentist drove.

"Really," said Gehring with a smirk. "What does your father do?"

"He's a longshoreman."

"And your mother?"

"She's a housewife."

"What kind of education did your parents have?"

I didn't know why he was grilling me this way; he hadn't done it to any of the other students. "Not much," I admitted. "They both had to drop out after ninth grade."

"Here we have it, class," Gehring announced loudly. "This is a typical example of a kid whose parents didn't finish high school and has little future himself. Carl will probably be a truck driver." Looking at me, he added, "That's about the only thing you'll be driving. Your Mercedes is nothing but a fantasy."

I was dumbfounded, which was lucky for me. The words I later wished I had said to him probably would have gotten me expelled. What the hell gave him the right to talk to me like that? And why the hell would he want to? I'd never done anything to the man.

The more I thought about it, the angrier I got. First off, what was wrong with being a truck driver? Why would he name that occupation as if it was somehow equivalent to being a failure? I'd bet there were a lot of kids in that school whose dads drove trucks for a living. There's nothing wrong with doing a blue-collar job. Growing up in a working-class family, I respected anybody who worked hard to make an honest living and provide for their children.

But worse, why would Mr. Gehring discourage a student from aspiring to go beyond that? What kind of teacher does such a thing? I had enough self-confidence that he couldn't discourage me, but what impact might this man have on another student?

I said nothing at the time, but I saw Mr. Gehring again a few years later and expressed myself more freely than I could have in his classroom. And what's more, I eventually got a Mercedes.

***

After the night of that dance with Bonnie, my father didn't put his hands on me again. However, there were several million other people in greater New York whom he still considered fair game. One of them was Newfield's dean of discipline.

My brother Anthony's priorities in high school were different from mine. He was all about having fun, and he relished the role of class clown. Schoolwork took a distant back seat to partying, playing pranks and pursuing girls. Anthony's sense of fun frequently conflicted with school rules, and he was regularly summoned to the dean's office.

One evening, when I was a senior and Anthony a sophomore, my father happened to be home at a normal dinner time. Throughout the meal, Anthony kept squirming in his seat and my father noticed it. "What's with you?" he demanded.

"Ah, I got in some trouble at school today. My butt's a little sore."

"*What*?"

"Mr. McCutcheon paddled me." McCutcheon was the dean of discipline.

"He did *what*?"

My brother repeated that he'd been paddled. Corporal punishment was legal at the time, generally accepted, and enthusiastically administered by Mr. McCutcheon.

"I'm going to your school first thing in the morning." My father waved his finger from Anthony to me. "The three of us. We're going in there together."

School didn't start until 7:30 and my father normally left the house at 4:30 for the docks. That meant he would be missing several hours of work. He did not like to miss work time, so I knew he was taking this very seriously.

The three of us walked into the main office promptly at 7:30. When the secretary saw me, she cheerfully said, "Good morning, Carl." When she spotted my brother, she sighed, "Hello again, Anthony." She politely asked my father, "May I help you?"

"Yeah, I'm looking for Mr. McCutcheon."

"Do you have an appointment?"

My father didn't answer. He had spotted McCutcheon's name on one of the office doors and made directly for it, with my brother and me trailing behind. Anthony appeared eager for whatever entertainment the encounter might provide. I was dreading the prospect.

Mr. McCutcheon was seated behind his desk and looked up with some surprise. He was a six-foot ex-Marine with a crewcut and a tough manner that intimidated every student at Newfield High School. But my father was not a student, and he sure wasn't intimidated.

My father went around the desk, grabbed Mr. McCutcheon by his throat, pulled him out of his chair and pinned him to the wall. He looked up at the taller man. "You touch one of my kids again and I will kill you. Nobody disciplines my children but me."

Anthony was almost bouncing up and down with excitement. "Go dad!"

I was terrified that this would get around the school and somehow the administration would retaliate against me. Certainly a parent threatening to kill an administrator couldn't be ignored.

Mr. McCutcheon responded with a choking sound.

My father went on, "I got three more kids coming up through this school and if I hear you touched any of them, I'm coming back here to see you." With that, he let go of the man's throat and led us out of the room.

I glanced back to see the dean struggling to catch his breath and looking more afraid than any kid who'd ever been sent to his office.

The story never did get around school. And none of the Bilancione kids were ever again touched by Mr. McCutcheon.

***

I had always worked whatever jobs I could get, even back in Brooklyn when my vicious Uncle Vito would hire me to help with his fruit truck. It's not that I was money-hungry, but I knew I would need cash to get through college. My grades might earn me a scholarship, but that would only cover tuition. I would still need finances for living expenses, transportation and the unexpected that always seem to pop up at the most inconvenient times.

To build up my college fund, I had a paper route that I completed before school every morning and worked weekends at Aggie's Deli. By my senior year of high school, I had a car—a decrepit '65 Oldsmobile 442 that a friend of my father's sold me for $150—so I could get a job beyond walking distance from home.

The job that I got was at a McDonald's, where I worked the register. The pay was minimum wage, of course, about $1.60 an hour. When I found out that McDonald's had a "#1 Club," that paid employees an extra ten cents an hour if they passed an exam, I prepared for that test as diligently as for a school exam and got the raise.

Another incentive the restaurant offered was a ten-dollar bonus for ringing up one hundred dollars of sales in one hour. A hamburger cost twenty-eight cents, a cheeseburger was a nickel more, and it was fifteen cents for a Coke. It took a lot of burgers and sodas to total a hundred dollars. But I could sum the items in my head, ring up the final amount and give the change quickly enough that I was racking up quite a few ten-dollar bonuses. Unfortunately, the management didn't really want to pay those bonuses and I was taken off the busy lunch and dinner shifts.

One day, our manager pulled a couple of other workers and myself aside to announce a surprise. He informed us that, as the restaurant's top employees, we would be going on an excursion to Greenwich, Connecticut, to see how the busiest McDonald's in the country operated. We would be traveling with Ray Kroc on his private bus. A trip to Connecticut might be nice, I thought, but for all I knew "Ray Kroc" could have been the bus driver. A couple of years later, I would recognize his name as the new owner of the San Diego Padres baseball team. But I didn't follow the business world in high school. My manager had to explain to me that Mr. Kroc was the owner and founder of McDonald's.

It was a relaxing trip in the most beautifully furnished bus I could imagine, just Mr. Kroc, the driver and three of us young guys from work. Mr. Kroc was a balding man of about seventy, dressed in a sharp-looking business suit. He was very courteous and chatted easily with us throughout the drive.

In Greenwich, I was impressed by the scale of the operation and how immaculate everything was. If a single French fry fell on the floor, it was picked up and the floor wiped clean within seconds. But I was only working at McDonald's to earn college money; I didn't find the burger business itself all that interesting.

It came as a surprise when Mr. Kroc asked to speak with me privately on his bus. I stepped aboard and he offered me a soft drink. I took a seat and he eased back into his leather recliner. "What are your future plans?" he asked me.

"I'm going to be a dentist."

He nodded thoughtfully. "Well, that's a good career. It will take a lot of years, though, and a lot of schooling."

"Yes, I'll be starting college next year."

"I'd like to make you an offer," he said. "I hear you're an excellent worker and a very bright young man. I like your personality and I like your energy. I could use a young man like you in my organization. What do you say I pay for you to attend Hamburger University and you come work for me?"

I thought it was a joke. There couldn't really be a school called Hamburger University. "You mean there's a school for flipping burgers?" I asked.

He chuckled. "No, no. Hamburger University is where we train our managers and corporate staff. It's in Illinois. I'll cover all your travel and living expenses."

So the offer was real, and it was very generous—but one in which I had zero interest. I told Mr. Kroc I was grateful for the offer and politely declined. He took it graciously and wished me well.

Later, I learned that graduates of Hamburger University actually receive a certificate that reads "Bachelor of Hamburgerology." I never regretted turning down Ray Kroc's offer. The only degree that would satisfy me was Doctor of Dental Medicine.

***

While I was in high school, my grandmother in Brooklyn died and my grandfather was alone. By now, the house on Bay 47th Street was in a trust in his children's names and he no longer owned it. My grandfather, always shrewd, convinced them to dissolve the trust and give him the house so that he'd have the security of that home for the rest of his life. As soon as they did, he sold the house and kept the money for himself. That meant he needed a place to live while he decided how to spend his windfall. After what he'd just pulled, none of my aunts and uncles would take him in. But, unhappily for us, my father did.

The bedrooms were all full, leaving only the living room couch for my grandfather's sleeping quarters. From there, he managed to cast his shadow over the entire house. My grandfather had always been mean and miserable, and his disposition had only gotten worse with the years. He was home all day, giving my mother endless orders and berating her for any failures. I was lucky; school, jobs and Bonnie kept me out of the house most of the time.

One morning, I was getting ready to do my paper route as usual. It was five o'clock, my father had left for work, my brothers and sister were still asleep, and my mother was in another room. My grandfather was eating the breakfast my mother had prepared for him. He looked at me and asked, "What do you work so hard for? I see you busting your ass every day."

"I need to make money for college."

"You really going to college?"

"Sure am."

He pushed his plate aside. "You know, not one of my kids or grandkids ever went to college—you'd be the first." He was thoughtful for a moment. "Tell you what: You get into college and I'll buy you a car."

I looked him in the eye and said coldly, "I would never take anything from you."

He appeared as startled as if I had slapped him. "I'm talking a Cadillac!"

"Not a goddamn thing." I grabbed my bag of newspapers and left to do my route.

It wasn't gracious of me, but I knew my grandfather. He was trying to buy his way into my good graces because he thought there might be something in it for him later on. I was not ever going to be in his debt, literally or figuratively.

He lived with us less than a year before moving to someplace in upstate New York. I don't recall exactly where, and I don't think any of us cared; we were all just relieved that he was out of our house.

***

By the end of senior year, I was enjoying life and optimistic about the future. Bonnie and I had been named "High School Sweethearts" by our classmates and it fit us perfectly. We remained a devoted couple, although she would be going on to Katherine Gibbs secretarial school and I had a choice of several colleges.

Among the scholarship offers I'd received was one from Stony Brook, an excellent university but located less than ten miles from Selden—much too close to home. I'd also had an offer from NYU, another outstanding institution, but I wanted an environment a bit less hectic than Manhattan.

The school I settled on was Fairleigh Dickinson in Teaneck, New Jersey. It was perfect for me. Without even requiring me to come in for an interview, FDU offered me a full academic scholarship. It also had an affiliated dental school nearby, and I assumed I could make a direct transition there after completing my undergraduate degree.

In the fall of 1973, I happily moved out of the family home in Selden and took another step toward a future of my own making.

4. Fairleigh Dickinson

How hard can it be to find New Jersey from New York? They're right next to each other! But I managed to get lost.

Since Fairleigh Dickinson hadn't required an interview, I had never visited the school and was unfamiliar with the route. I was crossing upper Manhattan in my battered Oldsmobile 442, which had more rust than paint and no front bumper. The seats were piled high with clothes, books and a care package from my mother. I wanted to get across the George Washington Bridge—not a difficult landmark to find—but took a wrong turn.

In the middle of Harlem, my car overheated and chugged to a standstill. I sat there and watched in disbelief as steam billowed up from around the hood. I didn't see any gas stations in the vicinity, and what I did see frankly worried me. In 1973, parts of Harlem were awfully scary and I was stuck in one of them. I slid down in my seat, doors locked, trying not to be seen and hoping not to crap my pants from fear. When the steam stopped rising, I figured the engine was cool enough to drive. Luckily, the car started and I had by now realized where I'd gone wrong in my navigation. This time, I found the bridge and crossed over to New Jersey. I pulled into the first service station I came to and filled my bone-dry radiator. With that, I was able to make it the next five miles to Fairleigh Dickinson University, on the east bank of the Hackensack River.

Once safely on campus, I transferred the contents of the Olds into my utilitarian dorm room. The dormitory was all-male, with a community bathroom and few amenities. It did have a hot-plate which allowed me to cook the prepackaged meals that my mother had given me.

Both my parents were helping ease my transition to college. Teaneck wasn't far from Bayonne where my father worked, and he would periodically come by and pick up my dirty laundry to take home. My mother would wash it and he'd bring it back to me along with another of her care packages—cans of Hi-C and boxes of macaroni and cheese were among the staples.

With my housing settled, I next got my schedule worked out. At Fairleigh Dickinson, pre-med and pre-dental students were assigned an academic advisor with a medical background. The advisor got me all set up with the courses I would need to fulfill the requirements for the pre-dental program.

Before I'd had my first class as a freshman, though, I was already looking across the river.

***

The College of Dental Medicine was housed in a beautiful, modern facility that had been built only a few years earlier. It was located on the Hackensack side of the river that separated it from Fairleigh Dickinson's main campus. I had barely begun my undergraduate studies when I crossed the bridge—more successfully than I had the George Washington—for an appointment with the dental school's director of admissions.

Dr. Howard Kimball was a former professor and a truly remarkable man. He had delayed his own entry into dental school so that he could serve as a gunnery officer on a Navy destroyer during World War II, winning commendations for his action in battles such as Iwo Jima and Okinawa. After the war, he completed his studies and established his own practice, only to be stricken with polio shortly thereafter. Now in his mid-fifties, he was confined to a wheelchair and headed the dental school's admissions office.

Dr. Kimball greeted me politely. "I'm very glad you're interested in applying," he said, "but it's a bit early. We don't begin accepting applications until November."

I was a *lot* early. "No sir, I'm not applying for next year. I'm just a freshman."

He appeared puzzled. "Then why are you here?"

"Because I want to know exactly what I need to do in college in order to be accepted when the time does come." I had no idea what the correct procedure was, but it made sense to me to learn this information as soon as possible. My goal was dental school and I thought of college as merely a stepping stone.

Dr. Kimball smiled slightly. "Well, you'll have to get good grades, of course. We don't look at anybody with less than a three-point-five grade point average. So work hard in your classes and keep an eye on your GPA."

Working hard and getting good grades were things I was accustomed to doing. I thanked him for his time and assured him that I would do as he'd advised.

***

Classwork went well my first semester, but I had little time for socializing. My scholarship paid for tuition and housing, but not books, food, transportation or any other expenses. The money I had saved during high school was fast dwindling and I had to earn more.

I started to leave campus as early as possible on Fridays to go back to Long Island and work at Aggie's Deli. I did the Friday night shift, then all day Saturday and Sunday, and I would leave Sunday night to be back at school for Monday morning classes. The driving and the work hours began overwhelming me, and I was looking forward to winter break when the campus would be closed for an entire month.

Two days before Christmas, I had my dorm room cleared out and my car packed for the trip home. When I tried to start it, the old Olds gave one harsh wheeze and died. I found a phone, placed a call to Bayonne and somebody tracked down my father on the docks.

"I don't know what to do," I told him. "I can't stay here because campus is shutting down today. And my car is completely dead." I knew it was beyond repair.

"I'll be there." Click.

My father soon arrived and we transferred the contents of my car to his. I thought he'd be taking me to Long Island, but instead he sped back to Bayonne. "I got a shift to finish," he said. "I'm not missing work hours because of you, mister."

That was fine with me; I was just grateful for the rescue.

Bayonne is a peninsula ideal for accommodating cargo ships. The docks jut out into Upper New York Bay from the

New Jersey side, within view of the Statue of Liberty and lower Manhattan.

I briefly wandered around one of the loading docks, amazed at the chaotic bustle. Cranes were swinging cargo from the ships onto the dock, forklifts were moving the larger containers, and hard-bitten men were manually carrying crates, sacks and bales with the hand-held metal hooks they wielded so skillfully. The noise was as chaotic as the movements, with horns, bells and whistles sounding nearby and echoing across the water.

I knew that the chaos made it easier for items to disappear from the dock. Much of the cargo never made it to its appointed destinations because men like my father redirected it elsewhere. The docks were like a distribution center for those mythical trucks from which so much merchandise kept falling.

I wasn't on the dock long before I got in the way of a burly longshoreman lugging an enormous burlap sack. He angrily shouted, "Get your ass inside, you damned fool," and I moved quickly to comply.

There was a break room in the main building where the men ate their lunches and hung out between shifts. While I waited for my father, I noticed a large bulletin board next to the refrigerator and idly began to scan the papers that had been posted. They weren't announcements of union meetings or warnings about following safety protocols, as I had expected. These postings were all about kids.

I knew that most of the longshoremen had little education and few resources. They were breaking their backs on the docks so that their children would have better opportunities. This bulletin board was where they boasted of their kids' successes. There was a school newsletter with a list of science fair winners and one of the names was underlined. A box score from a high school baseball game was nearby; the name of a boy who'd hit two home runs was circled. There was even a letter of acceptance from Notre Dame pinned to the board. And, to my astonishment, so were several of the report cards my father had silently stuck in his pocket. He was proud of me, and this was his way of bragging about me to his friends!

When my father finished his shift and came to get me, I didn't embarrass him by telling him what I had seen. But I rode back to Long Island feeling pretty good.

***

Christmas dinner included venison this year—the hunts were successful again now that I was no longer invited to join them—but my thoughts weren't on food. I was trying to figure out how I could continue college. I couldn't afford to attend without a job, I couldn't travel to a job without a car, and I didn't have enough money to buy a car.

My mother was especially concerned. Since I'd arrived home, she had asked me a half dozen times, "What are you going to do?"

When she asked the same question again after dinner, I announced my plan. "I'm taking this next semester off. I'll stay here and work at the deli until I can afford another car."

"You can't quit school!" my mother gasped.

"I'm not quitting," I assured her. "I'm putting it on hold. My first semester grades were good enough to keep my scholarship, and the school will freeze it for me until I'm able I go back."

I could tell from my mother's fretful expression what she was thinking. Often when something like school was put on hold, the hold could last forever. Life has a way of setting up detours and roadblocks that can keep you from ever getting back on track.

My father didn't comment at all. The next day, without a word, he went out. That wasn't unusual for him, but it seemed a bit odd that he would disappear while we were still celebrating the holiday, and we wondered about his absence.

He came back a few hours later, driving a 1971 Dodge Dart Swinger. It was gold with a mustard yellow interior. "That's your new car," he said, handing me the keys. "You're going back to school."

I was flabbergasted and tried to think of the words to thank him.

He waved off my thanks. "You owe me $2,200. Finish next semester, then work during the summer to pay me back. And you better have every cent of it by the time summer's over."

I promised that I would, vowing to work around the clock if necessary to pay him back on time.

Relieved at being able to continue school, I figured I could relax and enjoy the break that I so badly needed. Before starting college, I had carefully boxed up my precious baseball cards, magazines and scrapbooks and put them in a corner of the basement. I now had a few more Tom Seaver cards that I'd recently acquired and wanted to add them to the treasure trove. I was only halfway down the steps when I saw that the corner was empty.

I raced back into the living room. "Somebody moved my baseball stuff!"

My father answered gruffly, "Nobody moved it. I burned that pile of crap with the rest of the trash." I'd often seen him setting trash fires in the backyard and was horrified to imagine my baseball cards going up in smoke.

"*Why?*" I had spent years meticulously building and organizing that collection.

"Didn't want it cluttering up the basement."

Heartbroken, I went back down and stared at the corner where my collection had been. Then I went over to a spot behind the staircase where I had a glass terrarium. The previous summer, I'd gotten a couple of small boa constrictors and kept them in there as pets. My brother was in charge of their care while I was at college. The case was empty.

I ran up the stairs again. "Where are my snakes?"

My dad shrugged. "Killed 'em."

"But they were harmless!"

"We can't be looking after no animals for you."

I was devasted at the senseless loss of both the snakes and the baseball collection. But that was my father: He'd bail you out of trouble one day and commit an act of utter cruelty the next.

***

I completed spring semester with no difficulties and drove my Dodge Swinger back home to Selden. I'd already lined up several summer jobs so that I could earn enough to pay off the debt to my father.

Although I didn't quite work twenty-four hours a day, it sure seemed like it. On weekdays, I did landscaping for Bonnie's uncle from seven in the morning until four in the afternoon. Then I went home for a quick shower before going off to the pet store where I worked from five to eleven at night. On Saturdays and Sundays, I worked a third job putting in above-ground swimming pools. These were all minimum-wage positions, and $2,200 looked like a very distant goal.

One night, I came home from my late shift at the pet store, groggy from lack of sleep and fighting a summer cold. I overheard my mother say to my dad, "Rock, you've got to give Carl a break. He's worked *every day* this summer, even when he's sick." She tried to coax him, "Take a little off the price. Or at least give him more time."

"He owes me money," was his response, and my mother knew better than to press him further.

I continued to work every day until, with two weeks to spare, I handed my father twenty-two one-hundred-dollar bills. He counted them, folded them up and tucked the wad in his pocket. "Good," was the only word he said to me.

I was a bit disappointed at his response to all my hard work—I thought "nice job" or even a simple "thank you" would have been more appropriate. But I chose to look at the bright side: He had made it possible for me to continue school, he hadn't charged me a vig, and, since I'd paid on-time, he hadn't broken my legs.

***

At the start of my sophomore year, I made another appointment with the dental school's admissions director. I was determined to attend this institution and believed that regular visits would help pave the way for me.

When I entered his neat, well-appointed office, Dr. Kimball greeted me with a slight smile and quizzical expression. "What can I do for you today, Mr. Bilancione?"

I proudly reported, "I just wanted to let you know that I got the grades you said I would need for dental school."

Dr. Kimball offered me a seat. "We don't go by your *first year* grade point average. You still have three more years to go."

"Yes, but I'm sure I can do it." I'd gotten through freshman year and was confident that the rest of college would be smooth sailing.

"I hope you can," he replied. "But remember: Meeting the GPA requirement only means that we will *consider* your application."

I was a bit stumped. What more could there be besides grades?

He eased back his wheelchair and folded his hands. "Tell me what you do."

"Well, I work hard—both studying and jobs."

"That's it?"

"Pretty much. I don't really have time for anything else."

"Sports?

I shook my head no.

"School activities?"

Another no.

"Let me be frank, Mr. Bilancione: We're not looking for students like you."

I went from stumped to stunned. "I don't understand. You don't want students who work hard?"

"We don't want students who *only* work. We're looking for well-rounded individuals. A dentist deals with *patients*, not just teeth. You have to be able to interact with people, get to know them, discuss their interests. To do that, you need to develop some outside interests of your own."

What he said made perfect sense, but I didn't see how I could possibly do as he advised. I simply didn't have the time. Nevertheless, I thanked him for speaking with me and promised that I would try my best.

***

I had assumed that freshman year would be the toughest. For one thing, that's when students have to make the adjustment from living at home to the relative freedom and increased responsibilities of living on campus. There was also the jump in academic rigor from high school level to college. But for me, sophomore year turned out to be the real scholastic hurdle. The introductory classes of the first year were over with, and now it was on to the hard stuff.

Chemistry was the course that really kicked my butt. I simply couldn't figure out how to get a handle on the subject.

I finally asked the professor who the smartest kid in the class was, and he told me it was Richard Kelly, a brilliant young man who lived down the hall from me. I asked Richard if he would help me out and he readily agreed. That was one of the great things about our college: Most of the students didn't compete against each other, but rather tried help each other succeed. I was always happy to do the same when I had skills that I could share.

My academic work became strong enough that year that I was invited into the honors college, which allowed me to take any course that Fairleigh Dickinson offered. As a biology major, I also began a research project under the supervision of a doctoral candidate. We studied the effect that the hormone Prolactin has on growth. Although more work wasn't what Dr. Kimball had recommended, I figured contributing to a real research study would be a plus on my dental school applications.

As far as cutting down on my jobs and expanding my social activities, that was a greater challenge than chemistry. I couldn't reduce work hours and still afford the costs of going to college. Instead, I had to find a way to better manage my time and fit those hours into my daily school schedule.

One way I saved time was by staying on campus instead of going home to Long Island every weekend. I quit the jobs I had there and found employment at or near the school. I was briefly a cook in the school cafeteria, then got an early morning milk delivery route going from house to house dropping off orders and picking up empty bottles.

I also became a resident assistant of the dorm. As an R.A., I was responsible for maintaining a safe facility, checking that students complied with the rules and helping them with any housing issues.

Another position allowed me to include some sports in my life as well as earn a little money. I became president of the Inter-Dormitory Council and supervised all the inter-dormitory sports and activities for the students who lived on campus. In this role, I was in charge of the gym and was given a set of keys. I was only supposed to provide access for students, but I made an exception for a couple of the New York Yankees pitchers.

Fritz Peterson and Mike Kekich lived in Teaneck at that time. Peterson was a twenty-game winning All-Star and Kekich was... well, he was primarily known for his connection to Peterson. The two of them had recently scandalized much of America by their off-the-field activities. In the 1970s, wife-swapping was something of a vogue and they had taken it one step further by trading their entire families. Anyway, during the off season, they wanted to keep their throwing arms in shape, and I used to let them into the gym to work out.

I had accomplished a lot of what I'd set out to do that school year, but remaining on campus meant that I couldn't see much of Bonnie. Oddly enough, while I had moved out of the house in Selden, she had moved into it. Bonnie's evil stepmother had given her the boot and my family had taken her in. She shared a bedroom with my sister Janice and the two of them got along well. Everyone assumed that Bonnie would soon be an official part of the family, anyway.

Bonnie and I did more than assume: We got engaged.

***

When junior year began, I made my annual trip across the bridge to visit Dr. Kimball. I was still only half-way though undergraduate studies, and there was no reason for him to spend time with me, but he graciously granted me another appointment.

I proudly reported that I had maintained my grades while doing my best to become a more well-rounded person. I told him of my activities with the Inter-Dormitory Council, that I'd joined a bowling league, and that I had a girlfriend who was an executive secretary with the Muscular Dystrophy Association.

When I finished my account, he said approvingly, "I'm glad to hear you're doing so well, Mr. Bilancione. We'll look forward to receiving your application next year."

He didn't have any more suggestions, so I figured I was doing everything correctly and was a shoo-in for acceptance.

***

By my senior year, I was breezing through my courses and could devote much of my time to the application process for dental school. Although Fairleigh Dickinson's was the one I was fixated on attending, I thought it wise to cover my bases by applying to others as well. I ended up covering almost the entire country, sending out applications to sixty-two dental colleges throughout the United States. Application fees weren't very high back then; otherwise, I would have needed another job to pay for them all.

My transcripts and letters of recommendation were all good, and I had solid scores on my Dental Admission Test—a similar exam to the MCAT that pre-med students take for medical school. However, there was more to the process than paperwork. A lot of the dental schools required in-person interviews, and that would be a new experience for me.

Mrs. Dubin, for whom I'd worked on the Prolactin project, gently broached the subject with me. She was in her early forties, with gray hair pinned in a bun, and was well-versed in the protocols of academia. Mrs. Dubin explained to me that dental school candidates usually came from affluent, white-collar families and they would be dressed to the nines for their interviews.

I knew that I was different from most of my classmates; I saw them getting fancy new cars as birthday gifts and generous allowances so that they wouldn't have to work. I wasn't ashamed of my economic situation and simply asked her what I needed to do to compete.

"You need a nice suit," she said. "Go to Barney's—it's the best men's clothing store in New York." She began writing a list. "Ask for one of these."

She handed me the paper and I read the names: Bill Blass, Stanley Blacker, Christian Dior. I thanked her and planned a visit to Barney's in Manhattan.

My father decided that he would meet me at the store for the suit shopping. Neither of us had been to, or even passed, the store before and we were expecting a little shop like we might find in Bensonhurst. When he arrived, the two of us simply stood on the sidewalk for a few minutes, taking in the vast scale of the place. It was five-stories high and occupied the entire block of Seventh Avenue from 16th to 17th Streets.

We finally walked into the store, feeling like a couple of misfits in this upscale establishment. I was dressed as a scruffy 1970s college student, which is exactly what I was. My father had come directly from the docks, in his grimy work clothes with a pack of L&M cigarettes folded into the sleeve of his T-shirt. Although we were clearly out of place, the staff was as pleasant and courteous as could be.

A blonde who looked and dressed like a model was at the concierge desk. I went up to her and gave her my list of names. "I'm supposed to ask for one of these guys. Are any of them working today?"

She looked at the paper and smiled pleasantly. "I'll get someone to help you."

Soon a meticulously groomed young man approached. He wore an elegant suit with a silk pocket handkerchief. I checked the first name on my list. "Are you Bill Blass?"

"No, sir."

"Stanley Blacker?"

"I'm sorry, sir. There appears to be a bit of a misunderstanding." He explained very nicely that the names I had were designers, not salesmen. He added, "Quite understandable. It happens all the time."

I felt a bit foolish, but how was I supposed to know the names of fashion designers? I grew up in a neighborhood that was Ralph Kramden, not Ralph Lauren.

I told the salesman what I needed and he showed me a number of suits. With each one I tried on, I surreptitiously glanced at the sleeve to see the price and had to say, "This one isn't really me." He caught on to what the issue was and brought out some lower-priced suits. I finally settled on a Christian Dior that I thought made me look like a million bucks.

Before I went to the store's tailor to have my measurements taken, the salesman asked, "Would you care to accessorize?"

"I don't know what that is," I admitted. I certainly knew what an "accessory" was, but I don't think it was the kind that he meant.

He explained that he would choose a nice shirt and tie to go with the suit. I decided to let him pick those for me; he knew better than I did how to put an outfit together. Besides, compared to the suit how expensive could they be?

After I finished my fitting and we had our items, my father and I brought them to the cashier. My father surprised me by offering to pay for the tie and told the cashier to give him the bill for it.

When he saw the bill, he angrily told the clerk, "I said the *tie*, not the whole goddamn suit!"

"That *is* for the tie, sir."

I tried to let my dad off the hook. "I've been saving for this," I told him. "I can cover it."

He insisted he was a man of his word and paid for the tie. I knew it was a big expenditure for him and I was grateful that he wanted to help me make a good impression on my college visits.

I wore that suit, shirt and tie to every interview and on many other occasions for years to come.

***

The first dental school that accepted me was New York University. I was so excited that I went back to Newfield High School to share the news with my old guidance counselor Mr. Wallace. He had encouraged me throughout high school, never doubting that I would achieve my dream, and seemed almost as happy as I was at the news.

When I left his office, holding my acceptance letter from NYU, I spotted another familiar face in the hallway. It was Mr. Gehring, the English teacher who had humiliated me by announcing to the class that I would never be more than a truck driver. I walked right up to him and practically shoved the letter in his face.

I then gave him a few choice words, including a suggestion as to where he could put the letter. I also told him that if I ever heard of him trying to stomp on another student's dreams, I would come back to see him. I didn't go as far as my father had with Dean McCutcheon, but I got my point across. Mr. Gehring's face betrayed fear and embarrassment in equal portions and he made no reply. My sister Janice was in his class at that time and she later told me that my hallway confrontation with him was a shot heard round the school.

Mr. Wallace witnessed what happened and asked me to step back into his office for a minute. He said, "First, I'll never admit I said this, but I love what you just did. No teacher should belittle students the way Gehring likes to do, and I think you might have cured him of that. But do you know why he had it out for you in particular?"

I said I had no idea.

"Because you were telling everyone since the ninth grade that you were going to be a dentist. You were absolutely sure that you would make it."

"What's wrong with that?"

"Nothing at all. But you were a reminder to Mr. Gehring of his great failure in life. He originally wanted to be a dentist himself, but he was turned down by every dental school he applied to."

On hearing that, I almost felt badly for Gehring. Disappointment in his career plans was no excuse for taking his frustration out on students though.

***

More acceptance letters came in, including one from Columbia, as well as more invitations for interviews. But I'd heard nothing yet from my preferred dental school right across the river. Although I could get an excellent education at one of the other schools, my heart was set on Fairleigh Dickinson.

The deadlines to give the other schools notice whether I would attend or not were fast approaching and I was getting worried. I was about to contact Dr. Kimball, when I finally received the letter I'd been waiting for. It wasn't an acceptance, but it was an invitation to meet with him for a formal interview.

I confidently walked into Dr. Kimball's now-familiar office for the fourth time since I'd started college. His expression this time was harder to read. In the past, our meetings had been informal. For this occasion, he'd adopted a more business-like demeanor, almost stern.

He asked me what schools I'd applied to, and I told him.

"Have any of them accepted you?" he asked.

"Yes, several." I named some of the better ones.

"Those are good schools," he said approvingly. "You should go to one of them."

I was speechless. I had come to see him every year for four years to be sure I was on track to attend this dental school. Now he was telling me I should go elsewhere! When I found my voice again, I asked, "You mean instead of here?"

"Yes." He eased back in his seat and sadly shook his head. "You see, Mr. Bilancione, we don't find Fairleigh Dickinson students to be very good. We get much better applicants from other colleges."

I was dumbstruck. Fairleigh Dickinson's dental school didn't want students from Fairleigh Dickinson University? Why hadn't he told me that years ago?

Dr. Kimball noticed my distress and a twinkle came into his eye. "Make me proud," he said.

"You mean...?"

Having had his fun with me, he was smiling now. "You are the most persistent and passionate young man I have ever seen. You are *exactly* the kind of student we want here."

I don't think anyone has ever gone from crushed to elated as quickly as I did at that moment.

5. Across the Hackensack

The United States Navy almost scuttled my first year of dental school.

After receiving my acceptance letter from Fairleigh Dickinson's College of Dental Medicine, I applied for the Navy's Health Professions Scholarship. This scholarship would pay for dental school and provide me with an ensign's salary during my studies.

I submitted the required paperwork and was interviewed for the scholarship by Captain Hinrichs. He was an imposing figure, with a large and colorful ribbon rack on his chest. "Tell me about yourself," he said.

Never shy to do that, I gave him an account of my background, job history, academic achievements and career goals.

"I *love* this," he said. "You came up from the streets and you're determined to make something of yourself." He flipped through my application, transcripts and recommendations, and nodded approvingly. "This is terrific!"

"Thank you, sir."

Captain Hinrichs then reminded me of what I would owe the Navy in return. "You'll serve four years active duty in the Navy Dental Corps, and we can send you any place in the world we want to."

"I'm fine with that. They can send me anywhere." The prospect of seeing something beyond New Jersey and New York actually had a lot of appeal.

He shook my hand and assured me that I would be awarded the scholarship.

This was a huge relief. For the first time since PS 212, I wouldn't have to stress about having the money to continue my education. I could apply myself entirely to school without juggling a variety of jobs to survive.

I received my bachelor's degree in May, 1977. My parents both attended the graduation ceremony, as did my advisor Mrs. Dubin. There was no celebration party, but I didn't need one. The pride in my mother's eyes—visible even through her tears of joy—was the best graduation present I could have gotten. She had always believed in me and encouraged me to dream; now, we rejoiced together that this dream of a college education had been realized. My father kept his thoughts to himself; he didn't even say "Congratulations."

With college over, and thinking that I was all set for dental school, I allowed myself some vacation time—nothing extravagant, just a couple of road trips. The Navy might later send me off to see the world, but for now I was interested in getting a broader view of America.

I set off on a twenty-day cross-country drive with a couple of buddies. It was thrilling to see in person parts of the United States that I had only previously known from television or books.

The other road trip was with my fiancée Bonnie. Recently, we hadn't been able to spend as much time together as we would have liked since we went to different schools and both had jobs. We drove down to Florida and thoroughly enjoyed the sun and the beaches. After eight years together, we talked about when we might finally get married.

While we were in Florida, we visited my brother Anthony, who was now in the Marine Corps and assigned to the Naval Air Station in Jacksonville. After high school, Anthony had attended Suffolk County Community College on Long Island. He majored in criminal justice with the intent of becoming a police officer. After one semester, my father told him to give up college and enlist in the military. I think the issue was that my father would have been embarrassed if Anthony joined the police—in his view, it would have meant that he had a son on the wrong side of the law.

Rested from my summer fun, I was ready to face the rigors of dental school. I attended orientation and was eager for the semester to begin. Two days later, I was called into the financial aid office and informed that I hadn't yet paid my tuition. I explained to the clerk that I was on a Navy scholarship and asked her to check the records. She did. The scholarship had been given to another student.

I immediately went to a phone and called Captain Hinrichs to find out what had happened.

"It had to go to someone else," he said.

"Why? Did he have better grades?" If my scholarship had been pulled, I thought I was entitled to know why—especially since I hadn't even been notified of the change.

"I'm sorry, Carl," the captain said. "I'll be honest with you: It had nothing to do with merit. You absolutely deserve the scholarship. But the commanding officer of one of the naval training centers wanted it for his own son. He outranks me, and there was nothing I could do."

The captain sounded genuinely sympathetic, but that didn't lessen the devastating blow I'd just been dealt. He added, "I know I told you you'd get the scholarship, but I never put it in writing. So you can't hold me to what I said."

I learned a lesson from that: As far as the military is concerned, the word of an officer and a handshake aren't binding unless they're accompanied by paperwork. All I could do now was scramble for enough money to start classes.

***

Fortunately, I hadn't given up my position as resident assistant at the undergraduate dorms. This job came with a free room, relieving me of the cost of housing. Fairleigh Dickinson didn't have any housing on the dental school's side of the Hackensack, so I still would have had to live on the main campus anyway.

I applied for and received a government student loan at two percent interest, which covered tuition. For the rest of my expenses, I needed a job and found one at a nearby gas station. New Jersey gas stations provided students with a lot of employment. For some arcane reason, it was against the law for customers to pump their own gas in the state and there was always a demand for attendants.

With my tuition paid, I was able to begin the course work. It was grueling—much more intense than my undergraduate studies. First semester classes went from eight to five every day. They included biochemistry, immunology, pharmacology, gross anatomy, dental anatomy and dentures. We did everything from carve teeth out of wax to dissect entire human cadavers. There was far more to dentistry than I had imagined, and I was determined to learn it all.

My financial crunch was still a concern, so I telephoned Captain Hinrichs. He had previously mentioned another option with the Navy, and I thought it could be worth considering.

The captain again apologized for what had happened with the scholarship. "Look," he said, "I feel I owe you big time, so I'm going to make you an offer you're going to love." I was willing to listen, and he explained the details. "You join the navy now, but you won't be active duty until you graduate. And you'll only have to serve three years, not four. During one summer before graduation—you choose which summer—you'll go for an officer orientation course and you'll be paid $2,600. That's all the money you'll get until you go on active duty, but you'll be credited with four years experience which puts you at a higher pay grade. And your student loans will be deferred until after you finish your Navy service."

That was enticing. I knew I wouldn't be able to start my own dental practice immediately after school, so having three years Navy pay and my loans deferred would help a lot. I told him I would think about it.

"Let me sweeten it a little more," the captain went on. "I'll make sure you're stationed at Iwakuni, Japan. Every officer in the navy wants that assignment. You'll have off-base housing that comes with two Geisha girls. You know anything about Japanese culture?"

"Nothing at all."

"Well, believe me, you're gonna love it. The Geishas will treat you like a king."

I didn't care about Geishas, but I thought the financial arrangement would help me out and it would be interesting to see Japan. I soon called Captain Hinrichs back and accepted the offer.

When I went to Newark to sign the contract, I remembered how meaningless a verbal promise could be. I saw nothing in the document I'd been handed that specified where I would be stationed. I told the clerk that I wanted a clause added to the contract stating that I could choose my duty station.

"We don't do that," he said.

"Then I don't sign."

They inserted the clause, I signed and was inducted as an ensign into the United States Navy.

After the first semester, my college housing changed. I moved out of the dorm and into Bonnie's apartment in Maywood, New Jersey. In addition to the two of us finally being able to live together, there were several other dental students in the same apartment complex and we formed a study group. One of the members of this group later proved important to my future, but not because of our dental studies.

***

I attended Officer Indoctrination School, as it was then called, in Newport, Rhode Island, between my first and second years of dental school. I knew it would be like summer camp compared to the Marines' basic training that my brother had had to endure at Camp Lejeune. All I was being trained for was how to act like an officer in the Navy Dental Corps. I was never going to be put at the helm of a battleship.

I arrived at OIS with long hair, a beard and a bowling ball. Another student from Fairleigh Dickinson carried a bag of golf clubs. The Navy got rid of the excess hair pretty quickly, but failed to convince me that I wasn't on vacation. Nobody told me—or perhaps I hadn't been paying attention—that we weren't supposed to leave the grounds without permission. I believe I set a record with twenty-six Unauthorized Absences, never once getting caught. I drove back to New Jersey almost every weekend to see Bonnie. I also regularly went off base to go bowling with a group of Navy SEALs. That came to an end when the SEALs learned that I was an ensign. They were enlisted men and prohibited from fraternizing with an officer.

As with any other school I'd attended, I was conscientious about my classwork and performed well on my tests. These covered Navy history and traditions, military etiquette and the many details involved in properly wearing a uniform.

After eight weeks, I had completed the required officer training and was given a check for twenty-six hundred dollars. However, I no longer had a fiancée.

When I returned from Newport, Bonnie told me that she wanted to put our engagement on "hold." We still loved each other, we hadn't fought, and neither of us was involved with anyone else. I think she simply sensed that our lives were going in different directions and that we were growing apart. I was stunned at first—we'd been together for nine years at this point—but came to realize that she was probably right. By the next day, the engagement had gone from "hold" to "off."

It seemed I was always gaining something and losing something. I had the money from the Navy to begin sophomore year and another job lined up to carry me through it. But I had no girlfriend, and, since I'd been living in Bonnie's apartment, I was now homeless.

***

I began sophomore year living in a rented room in someone's home, until I found a better solution. I'd had training as a phlebotomist and was working at the Paramus Blood Bank drawing blood from donors. This blood bank had a two-bedroom apartment attached, which was reserved as housing for the two student workers with the most financial need—and I certainly qualified as one of those. A condition for living in the apartment was that at least one of the students had to be on call from 6 pm to 7 am Monday through Thursday as well as on weekends. In addition to our regular work in the blood bank, we had the option to deliver the needed blood products to hospitals in the Metro New Jersey-New York area. That provided extra pay, and the blood bank supplied the cars and the gas. Having a job and housing in the same place was convenient, and I was fine with the hours.

My roommate in the apartment was Pete Capone, a great guy but not big on cleanliness. We became known as Oscar and Felix because he was a slob and I was a neat freak. Pete's father was an auto mechanic on Long Island, but he was also a younger brother of "Scarface" Al Capone, so Pete was Al Capone's nephew. I felt a little bad for Pete because everybody was always asking about his name and making gangster jokes. If you have an Italian last name, people often assume you're related to Mafiosi. In Pete's and my cases, it happened to be true, but neither of us had anything to do with that life. We were both honest, hard-working guys trying to make our way through dental school.

A few months into the semester, I was studying in the library when Steve Nagy, a friend from the study group at Bonnie's apartment building, came over to me. He was accompanied by a very attractive young woman with long blonde hair who was dressed all in white. Steve introduced us. She was Deborah Schlussler, an education major who was considering switching to the dental hygiene program. We chatted briefly, they left, and I went back to my studies.

Steve called me that night. "What did you think of Deborah?" he asked.

"She seemed nice."

"Well, she liked you and she's hoping you'll ask her out."

She and I had barely spoken, but I was open to the idea of a date and told him so. I didn't learn until later that, after he got off the phone with me, he called Deborah with the same spiel.

This was 1978, and Linda Goodman's astrology book *Love Signs* was on the best-seller lists. Steve liked to do horoscopes and according to Goodman's book he discovered that Deborah and I had our planets aligned or our moons on a cusp or something like that. So he manipulated us into a date in order to facilitate whatever destiny he believed the stars had ordained for us.

Our first date was just before Christmas. I'd scraped together all the cash I had on hand—thirty dollars—to take her to a trendy disco, the New York Connection in Fort Lee, which had no admission fee.

When we ordered our drinks, I discovered that they made up for the lack of a cover charge with exorbitant drink prices. Deborah ordered a Pink Lady, which was five dollars. I had a gin and tonic, figuring it would be one of the cheaper options—another dollar seventy-five. Alright, I figured, as long as we didn't start chugging them I should have enough to get through the night.

We'd barely started talking when I saw that Deborah's glass was empty and another Pink Lady was on the way. I nursed my gin and tonic, and despite the loud music we had a great conversation. Among other things, we spoke about our families. Deborah grew up in Lincroft, New Jersey, the middle one of three children. Her father was an electrical engineer with a number of patents; he served as a civilian chief engineer at the Fort Monmouth Army base. Deborah was interested in following her mother's career path and becoming a teacher.

As the conversation went on, I was impressed with how bright and personable Deborah was. Yet I was somewhat distracted by the growing bar bill I was tallying in my mind. What was I going to do if my money ran out? That would be a horrible embarrassment. Just as I was doing some mental calculations, Deborah downed her entire cocktail and went to the ladies' room again. When she came back, we decided it was time to leave. I didn't want the date to end, but since it coincided with my cash being exhausted the timing worked out perfectly.

I had to laugh when I learned later what had happened. Deborah didn't care for the taste of alcohol, so she had been spitting her drinks out. She'd only ordered them to look sophisticated. I had tried to impress her by taking her to a club I couldn't really afford, and she had tried to impress me by ordering fancy cocktails that she didn't really want to drink!

***

Our second date had to wait until the new year. Deborah already had vacation plans in Cozumel for the winter break, and I had to put in as many work hours as I could get. Once she came back, however, we were dating regularly and exclusively. I met her parents, who were marvelous people, and we all got along splendidly.

Shortly before spring break, Deborah asked me where I'd be going during the time off. Most of the students either went skiing or to Fort Lauderdale. I had to tell her that my vacation would be spent closer to home, studying for sophomore boards at the library and pumping gas at the service station.

Deborah's friends had invited her to join them on a trip to Ft. Lauderdale. When she heard I'd be staying home, she turned them down, sacrificing her vacation to spend the break with me. She sat with me in the library while I studied and cooked us meals before I went to work. We grew even closer during that time, and I think we had a more enjoyable spring break than the students who went to Vail.

Deborah was smart, attractive and had the kindest heart of anyone I'd ever known. I loved her, and by the end of the school year I knew that this was the woman I wanted to spend my life with.

***

There probably aren't a lot of dentists who can say this, but my first patient was a murderer. In fact, so was my first assistant.

Dental students typically don't work on patients until their third year, but I was given a chance to start early. Fairleigh Dickinson announced a summer externship between second and third years in which qualified students would perform a full range of dental work on real live patients. Very few students applied for the position. For one thing, most of them had vacation plans they didn't want to cancel. Also, there would be no pay; it was strictly voluntary. Finally, the patients would be inmates of the high-security federal penitentiary in Lewisburg, Pennsylvania, and the treatments would be done inside the prison.

Lewisburg housed some of the most violent men in America, including a number from my old neighborhood in Brooklyn. It was almost a second home to wiseguys from the New York families. This was where the real gangsters from the movie *Goodfellas*—Henry Hill, "Jimmy the Gent" Burke, Tommy DeSimone and Paul Vario—served their time. A section of one of the cell blocks was known as "Mafia Row," and they ruled it pretty much the way it was portrayed in the film. John Gotti and Anthony "Tony Pro" Provenzano also served time there, as did Whitey Bulger of the Boston mob and Jimmy Hoffa. Lewisburg could even boast of Al Capone, Dutch Schultz and Enoch Johnson—immortalized as "Nucky Thompson" in *Boardwalk Empire*—among its more illustrious alumni.

I was eager for hands-on experience, and not unfamiliar with criminals, so I readily agreed to go. My classmate Paul and I were the only two students to be accepted into the program. Fairleigh Dickinson made the arrangements with Lewisburg, and we headed out to central Pennsylvania.

Paul and I were housed in a budget motel near the penitentiary. We had our meals in the mess hall, eating the regular fare served to prisoners. Lewisburg had its own vegetable gardens and the food turned out to be quite good—much better than some of the meals I'd had in college.

When I first arrived at the prison, I thought it was the strangest place I'd ever seen. The old-style facility, built in the 1930s, appeared completely out of place amidst the scenic, quiet farmland that surrounded it. The architecture was odd, too. As expected, there were brick walls, barbed wire fences and towers with armed guards. But somebody had stuck a gothic façade on the main building as if trying to disguise it as Notre Dame cathedral.

The walk to the prison's medical clinic was an ordeal. It was only possible to proceed a short distance before coming to a closed steel gate. I'd have to stop, wait for the gate behind me to close and the one in front to open, then progress again to the next barrier. And with every step, I was being eyeballed by the inmates and subjected to their incessant cries of "Fresh meat! Fresh meat!"

As students, our work was to be supervised by Lewisburg's full-time dentist, Dr. DeVos, and we were assigned a couple of prison trustees as dental assistants. But we received little guidance from DeVos, an ungainly man of about forty, who stayed in his office while we treated the patients. He gave us only two instructions: "Don't leave any pens around" and "Don't talk to the prisoners, especially not the assistants." The pens, of course, could be put to a number of uses in a prison besides writing. I was a bit careless at first and a couple of mine disappeared before I became more vigilant. As far as not talking, anyone who knows me knows that's an impossibility.

My assistant was Tony, a handsome African-American, about six-foot-four with a powerful build, a ready smile and an engaging personality. We chatted frequently. Inevitably, I asked him what he was in for, and he answered, "Murder." Tony explained that he wasn't really a murderer, though, because he had only done it once and the guy had it coming. I chose not to ask him how many people one had to kill to qualify as a "murderer."

Paul's assistant was Benny the Cuban. He told me he was in prison because of his "retirement portfolio." He had trafficked millions of dollars worth of cocaine in Miami. When he was arrested, the police had gotten his drugs, but not his money. All he had to do was finish his prison time, retrieve his fortune and enjoy a happy, lavish retirement.

Both men were considered model prisoners and so had been given the coveted jobs in the dental clinic. They earned ten cents an hour, which was credited to their prison accounts and allowed them to buy snacks and other luxuries at the commissary. Although I received no pay, I was gaining valuable experience—and lots of it.

Every day, there was a line of inmates outside the clinic door waiting for treatment. I asked Tony if it was always so busy, and he told me prisoners held off on their dental care until the students arrived each summer. They wanted to avoid being treated by Dr. DeVos. "He treats us like animals," said Tony. I had noticed that the dentist was lacking in technical ability and had even worse social skills.

In a civilian practice, Dr. DeVos wouldn't have lasted six months before malpractice suits put him out of business. So here he was in a federal job, doing shoddy work on men who had no recourse against bad treatment. What was truly unforgiveable, though, was the fact that he seemed to take pleasure in making the prisoners suffer. I had the impression that he'd probably been bullied in school and was now enjoying some kind of revenge against tough guys.

I witnessed his sadistic streak myself when I was doing a root canal on an inmate. The prisoner was in shackles and a guard stood next to him, shotgun at the ready. The procedure was going well, but I had to focus intently on my work since I was so new to it. I almost jumped at a tap on my shoulder. It was Dr. DeVos. "Time for lunch," he said.

"Can't," I replied, without looking up. "I need to finish this. I already have the nerve exposed."

"The hell with him. It's lunch time."

Now I did look up—in disbelief. "I can't leave him with his tooth open like this," I said. "The anesthesia will wear off and he'll be in agony."

"Not my problem. He's an animal anyway."

At this, the prisoner lunged for DeVos and the guard sharply butted the man in the head with his shotgun. More guards hustled into the room and the prisoner was taken away.

When I recovered from the shock, I asked Dr. DeVos, "What's going to happen to him? His tooth is still open—the pain is going to be excruciating."

DeVos was getting annoyed with me. "Look, you have to remember something: These men are *prisoners*. So knock it off with the compassion crap. They don't deserve it."

Not long after, Tony mentioned to me that the inmates were planning to cut Dr. DeVos's throat. It did not sound like an idle threat. Without revealing who had told me, I warned DeVos.

"They've been plotting against me for years," he said, with no indication of concern. "Nothing ever comes of it."

I also reported what I'd heard to the prison authorities. They, too, dismissed it as "just talk."

Two months after I returned to Fairleigh Dickinson, Dr. DeVos had his throat cut from ear to ear. He survived, but barely, and his sorry career at Lewisburg was over.

***

I was now halfway through dental school, but my mind was less than half on dentistry. For the first time in years, I had something more important to consider than getting my D.M.D. degree: I wanted to marry Deborah.

It was wrong of me, but I neglected to ask Deborah's parents for permission first. I believe I should have shown them that respect. Instead, I discussed it with my father.

We met at a diner in Bayonne near the docks where he worked. I later found out that this was where his mistress worked—for all I know, she might have been our waitress. So I was asking marriage advice from a man who was violating his own vows.

I told him that I was thinking of proposing to Deborah.

"How do you feel about her?" he asked. "Do you love her?"

"With all my heart. She is so wonderful, so supportive—the nicest woman I've ever been with." Then I mentioned the potential sticking point for my family. "But she's not Italian."

He shrugged it off. "Who cares? I married your mother and she's not Italian. Go ahead and marry the girl."

I was happy at his response, although I would have proposed to her with or without his approval.

To have the right setting for popping the question, I took Deborah to a restaurant in Atlantic Highlands. It was a romantic place right on the water, and served some of the best seafood in New Jersey.

We had just ordered our dinners, when I blurted, "Would you marry me?"

My tone must have made it sound like a hypothetical question. Deborah answered casually, "Yeah, I suppose I would."

I had to try again. "What I mean is... I'm *asking* you to marry me."

"Oh!" She appeared stuck for a response. Finally, she said, "Yes, I will."

I was about to tell her how happy she'd made me when she abruptly got up from the table and ran out. I wondered if she'd suddenly changed her mind.

The waiter arrived with our food and noticed her rush to leave. "What happened?" he asked.

"I don't know, but I think I might have really botched things." I was trying to figure out exactly where I'd gone wrong.

It was a huge relief when Deborah came back to the table and explained that she'd hurried to phone her parents and tell them the good news. After dinner, we went to her parents' house, and they warmly welcomed me into the family.

The next day, we went to pick out an engagement ring. I took Deborah into Manhattan, where my friend Jerry worked in the Diamond District. Coincidentally, Jerry's wife had been my first patient who was not a convicted felon.

Jerry was an excellent jeweler with a clientele that included Frankie Valli of the Four Seasons and Lawrence Taylor of the New York Giants. He made sure we got an excellent stone at a price that I could afford.

Deborah and I were married on July 27, 1980, at the Ridgefield Catering Hall in Verona, New Jersey. Her mother planned a magnificent formal wedding for us. There were 125 guests, including Deborah's family, my family, and a contingent from New York's Five Families. My father hired the Herb Rose Orchestra for the occasion. Sally Provenzano, a singer and the wife of my father's best friend, performed a beautiful rendition of *Can't Help Falling in Love*. I had been planning to surprise Deborah by singing that very song, but Sally beat me to it. After hearing her voice, I was glad she did! Following the reception, Deborah and I left for our honeymoon in Acapulco.

***

During my senior year, Captain Hinrichs called to remind that I would be reporting to the Navy after graduation. When I mentioned that I was now married, he angrily let loose with some of the language for which sailors are so famous. From the way he went on, my getting married was a worse act of betrayal than spying for the Soviets.

Furious, he said, "You can forget about Japan! I'm sending you to Great Lakes!" Naval Station Great Lakes was the most dreaded assignment in the Navy. Located on Lake Michigan in northern Illinois, it was home to the Navy's only actual boot camp and was referred to by those in the service as "Great Mistakes."

I calmly replied, "No, you're not."

After another spectacular string of profanity, he said, "I can send you anyplace I want to, and you're *going*. You've got a contract, mister."

"Yes, and my contract says I can choose where I'm stationed."

"Bullshit!" He hung up.

A little time passed, during which Hinrichs must have read the contract I'd signed and seen the clause that I'd had inserted. He called me back. "Alright smartass, where do you want to go?"

"Orlando." Deborah and I had taken a trip there to visit her brother, and we thought Florida would be a nice place to live.

"*Everybody* wants Orlando. We have all the dentists we need at that base. Pick someplace else."

"Orlando."

I don't think the captain ever had to comply with an order from an ensign before, but he got me assigned to the Naval Training Center in sunny Orlando.

I breezed through my final months at Fairleigh Dickinson, ecstatic that all these years of schooling were finally over. At graduation, along with my diploma I received an honor that I didn't even know existed. During dental school, I had done a lot of volunteer work treating special needs children. In recognition of this, I was given the New Jersey State Pediatric Dentistry Award. Once again, my mother struggled to hold back tears of pride.

Now, finally, I could put into practice the skills that I had learned, and Deborah and I could start a family. In 1981, I left New Jersey with a loving wife, a Doctor of Dental Medicine degree, some wonderful memories—and a three-year commitment to the United States Navy.

6. Lieutenant Bilancione, USN

I was sure that I would come to enjoy living in Orlando—if I didn't starve first.

Shortly after Deborah and I moved to Florida, I asked a neighbor, "What's the best Italian restaurant in Orlando?"

His reply was, "The spaghetti and meatballs at Denny's is pretty good."

I laughed, assuming he was joking. He wasn't.

I thought wistfully of the holiday meals my grandfather used to cook in his basement. I had the feeling it might be a long time before I'd be enjoying parmigiana di melanzane or pasta fagioli e cozze again.

Surely there had to be some good pizza in the area, at least, so I asked someone else for the name of the city's best pizzeria.

"Pizza Hut."

I sighed. Never mind yearning for my grandfather's cooking, by now I was starting to have fond memories of the prison meals at Lewisburg.

Deborah wasn't faring any better in her attempts to find the foods we wanted. She had gone to the nearest supermarket for bagels, lox and cream cheese, which she wanted to surprise me with for Sunday breakfast. She asked a clerk at the deli counter, "Can I get some lox, please?"

The clerk came out from behind the counter and led her to an aisle where there was a small hardware section. He pointed to the combination locks hanging on a hook.

"I mean the *fish* lox," she explained.

He looked at her as if she was crazy. "There's no fish named 'locks.'"

She tried to convince him. "It's salmon—cured, sliced thin. People eat it on bagels."

"We don't have nothing like that." The clerk still seemed to think that Deborah had taken him on a snipe hunt.

When she came home, Deborah told me about her fruitless quest for lox and asked, "What kind of a place did you bring me to?"

***

When Deborah and I drove down from New Jersey in the summer of 1981, we arrived at an Orlando that wasn't yet the sprawling city it grew to become. Its population was no more than that of a "neighborhood" in Brooklyn and a good percentage of its residents were military families.

Until Walt Disney came along, McCoy Air Force Base had been Orlando's largest employer and an important defense facility. Pilots trained there during World War II, U-2 spy planes flew out of McCoy on reconnaissance missions during the Cuban missile crisis, and it served as a base for the Strategic Air Command, which was responsible for some of the country's nuclear strike forces.

After the Vietnam War, the Air Force installation had been shut down and part of the site redeveloped as Orlando International Airport, which retained McCoy's airport code "MCO." Now, instead of spy planes and bombers, the passenger jets of Eastern Airlines, billed as "the official airline of Walt Disney World," dominated the skies.

As for Walt Disney World, it consisted of only a single park, Magic Kingdom, and admission cost eight dollars. There was a bit of a furor when the ticket price shot up to $9.50 later in the year.

While the air base was being phased out, the Naval Training Center was expanding, taking over some of McCoy's grounds and buildings. Along with about sixteen other first lieutenants beginning their active duty with the Navy Dental Corps, I was scheduled to start my service on August first. Deborah and I had arrived early in our tightly-packed Honda Accord, and there was no housing available for us yet.

We spent our first two weeks living with her brother Dick. He was a bachelor with a cluttered one-bedroom apartment not far from the base, and he allowed us to sleep on his pit couch. Dick wasn't around much, so Deborah and I were free to explore the area on our own.

When officer housing became available, we moved into a small house, identical to all its neighbors, on the site of the old Air Force base. It was large enough for Deborah and me to live comfortably, but the uniformity of every structure, and the innumerable rules that governed their maintenance, kept it from feeling like it was our home. Then again, it wasn't—the house was property of the Defense Department and every detail was determined by the military.

New lieutenants in the Navy Dental Corps were assigned to the "amalgam line." All we did was fill the cavities of recruits who were undergoing basic training. It was like being on a production line. We were expected to drill, fill, and call for the next recruit to take the chair. It was not the way I had imagined practicing dentistry. I'm an independent-minded person, and it wasn't long before I doubted whether my relationship with the service would be an enduring one.

***

The housing situation got to me first. Every Saturday, the Navy sent a persnickety enlisted man to perform an inspection of the officers' neighborhood. He went to every house with a ruler, measuring the height of the grass and whether cars parked in the driveway were the appropriate distance from the edge of the lawn. In addition, he walked around each home to be sure that no windows were open, and checked for compliance with a multitude of other rules and regulations. This guy was stricter than the petty officers who were conducting uniform inspections in the nearby boot camp!

After only two months of Navy accommodations, I petitioned my commanding officer for permission to live off base. Deborah and I both knew that we wouldn't be happy continuing to live under the scrutiny of a military functionary. She had already gotten a job as office manager for a dental practice in the Jefferson Ward department store on the west side of Orlando. Between our two salaries we thought we could afford to get a small place of our own.

While we awaited the decision on my housing petition, Deborah and I began taking advantage of the many opportunities to explore nature in central Florida. The Italian cuisine in the area might have been lacking, but the lakes, rivers, beaches and wildlife were breathtaking. We especially appreciated the "Old Florida" that still existed—pristine wetlands inhabited by a colorful variety of birds, waterways where we could kayak among the manatees, and hiking trails through woodlands that dripped with Spanish moss. Alligators were ubiquitous; our first encounters with them were a little scary, but they never threatened us and we soon accepted them as just another fascinating creature making Florida its home.

On any weekend that we could get away, we drove to Shepard Park in Cocoa Beach where we could swim in the ocean and enjoy a basket lunch at a picnic table. Deborah likes to fish, so sometimes we would go Port Canaveral and set out with thirty or so other people on a charter boat to do some nighttime bottom fishing.

I also began scuba diving, taking lessons from Hal Watts, a world record diver who later explored such famous wrecks as the Civil War ironclad Monitor and the Andrea Doria. Under his instruction, I became Advanced Open Water certified and dove to a number of fascinating sites myself.

On weekdays, I was still doing an endless number of routine fillings and was itching to break free from the amalgam line. I approached the captain in charge of the endodontics department and asked if I could work for him; he agreed, and I performed a number of root canals under his supervision. Like the other department heads, he was board certified in his specialty and had excellent clinical skills. When I'd learned what I could from him, I went to the captain who ran the oral surgery department and was accepted there. After that, it was periodontics for a while, then prosthodontics. I made my way through every department, directed by some of the finest dentists I'd known, learning new techniques and expanding my skill set.

But by now I was certain that I wasn't going to make the Navy my career. I had great respect for the institution, appreciated the fine work that my colleagues performed, and certainly intended to give the service my best efforts while I was on duty. However, I needed to go my own way and be my own boss.

***

When I received permission to live off base, Deborah and I looked around for a house that we could afford. We settled on a one-story spec house on Margarita Drive, not far from the University of Central Florida. It was a new development of forty homes, and we were the first to move in. I didn't know how we would ever come to own it, though. The thirty-year mortgage carried a sixteen percent interest rate, and it would be many years before we could pay down the principal. Still, although the bank was the true owner, we made the place our own and relished the freedom and pride that came with it.

At the training center, my independent streak was putting me at odds with the Navy brass. A recruit from Texas came into the clinic, and I saw that he had no enamel on his front teeth—this is a condition that some people are born with. I proposed capping six of his teeth with porcelain crowns.

The captain in charge of prosthodontics called me into his office. "What the hell is this?" he demanded, waving the treatment plan I'd submitted. "You want to give crowns to a *recruit*?"

"Yes, sir. He doesn't have any enamel on his teeth. They'll rot away as they are."

"I know that—but it's not the Navy's problem. We don't put *any* crowns on recruits, never mind *six*!"

I repeated that my proposal was the correct approach for the young man's problem.

As a dentist—and he was a good one—I think the captain knew I was correct. But as a Navy officer he was bound by protocols. "Look," he said, "we don't even know if he'll make it through basic training. Suppose you do the work and he washes out? He goes back home with a nice set of crowns compliments of the U. S. Navy, and we get no service time out of him."

"But it will save his teeth," I persisted. "And he seems like a good recruit—I'm sure he'll make it through."

The captain studied me for a minute. "Six crowns is a lot of work. Are you certain you're capable of doing something that extensive?"

"Yes, sir."

He nodded thoughtfully. "Very well, go ahead." I was dismissed and turned to go. When I reached the door, he added, "One more thing Lieutenant Bilancione: If he washes out, you're dead."

I scheduled the work on the recruit, but before I allowed him to sit in the chair I told him, "Write down your home address for me, because if you don't make it through basic I'm going to come looking for you."

The procedure went well, the crowns fit beautifully and I was summoned to see the commanding officer. He immediately ripped into me for having done six crowns on a recruit, pointing out what a waste of Navy resources that had been. He was so angry, I had the feeling that he was contemplating sending me to the brig.

I was standing there taking his abuse silently when my captain walked in. He ordered me to leave the office. I didn't know what to do. The CO had told me to come in, and he outranked the captain, so which order was I supposed to obey? The captain repeated his order, louder, and I followed it.

There was no need to send me out of the office, though, since I could clearly hear the yelling through the door. I don't know how he got away with it, but the captain told the CO in no uncertain terms not to meddle in his department. He said that I'd had his permission to do the crowns and that I'd done a great job. The captain came back into the hallway, gave me a curt nod, and that was the end of the matter. Well, not quite the end—the recruit made it through basic training and could smile brightly when it was over.

***

Moving into our home on Margarita Drive was but the first step away from the Navy. Next, I applied to take the exams for a license to practice dentistry in Florida. This would qualify me to work outside of the military anywhere in the state—and I definitely had private practice in mind. I had passed the Northeast Regional Boards in New Jersey, but Florida had its own certification exams.

I received permission to take the Florida boards, passed them, and immediately submitted another request to moonlight during my off-duty hours. The commanding officer asked why I wanted an outside job. I explained that I needed the extra income—I had a mortgage to pay, and Deborah and I were planning to start a family. I also admitted that I wasn't sure I'd be making the Navy my career anyway. I don't think the last point came as any surprise to him—in fact, it might have been a relief—and he granted my request.

I soon found an established dentist who was willing to hire me. His name was Dr. Antonio Sanchez, and he had been Cuban dictator Batista's personal dentist until Fidel Castro came into power.

Dr. Sanchez's close affiliation to the exiled military dictator made him an "enemy of the revolution" in Cuba. His wife and children had been able to flee the country, but Dr. Sanchez's home and property were all confiscated and he was jailed. He spent about five years in prison before he was able to engineer a successful escape. After a brief stay in Miami, he traveled to Orlando where he settled and reunited with his family. Fortunately for Dr. Sanchez, he had been involved in joint programs between the American Dental Society and the Cuban Dental Society prior to the revolution. The ADS had copies of his credentials and he was able to go into practice in the United States.

I put in as much time at Dr. Sanchez's practice as my duties at the Naval Training Center would allow. Soon I was treating half the patients in his office, and the extra money I was earning almost matched my Navy pay. Feeling more affluent than we actually were, I took out an auto loan for a new Datsun 280Z sports car which the other officers saw me driving back and forth to the base.

Life was getting better and better for us. Deborah and I were putting down roots, doing well professionally and establishing some strong friendships. Best of all, Deborah was pregnant and we were looking forward to our first child.

***

My happy life was going too well for the Navy's liking, however. With about a year left to go in my enlistment, I was called into the commanding officer's office where several of the captains I'd worked for were already seated.

"Lieutenant Bilancione," the CO began, "you are one of our brightest stars. You've done an outstanding job in every department you've served."

"Thank you, sir." I braced myself for what might be coming—the CO did not summon junior officers in order to give them compliments.

"We all agree that your abilities are truly exceptional." At that, the other captains nodded. "And because you're so good, we've decided that you've outgrown us and need to move to a larger playing field. In two weeks, you're shipping out to Okinawa."

"*Okinawa*?" I repeated in a nonmilitary squawk.

He nodded. "That's a very important assignment. The United States has a dozen military bases on Okinawa and you'll be busy at a number of different facilities. It will be quite career step for you."

I didn't *want* a career step. My career wasn't going to be in the Navy, and I thought that was obvious to everyone. "But sir, my wife is pregnant."

"She won't be going with you. You'll be able to see her again when your tour of duty ends."

"That's a year away."

"Yes. Dismissed."

Deborah cried all night when I broke the news to her. "It's because of your big mouth," was her assessment. "You keep telling everybody how much better life is *outside* the Navy. So now they're punishing you—and me."

She had a point. I was the only dentist in my class who had a home off the base, the only one moonlighting in private practice, and my new sports car was an eye-catcher. The Navy brass wanted to retain its officers and I'd been flaunting the fact there was a terrific life to be had outside of the service. Although I'd had permission for all my extracurricular pursuits, I was a bad example to the other lieutenants because they might consider leaving the Navy, too.

It also didn't help that whenever there was a conflict between my proposed treatment plan and the Navy's way of doing things, I would say, "I'm a dentist first, and an officer second." As far as the military was concerned, I had my priorities backwards.

I considered my predicament and came to believe that the captains didn't really want my service in Okinawa. Their goal was to punish me for being so blatantly non-military. The Navy had the right to ship me out, since the contract I'd signed in Newark only gave me the choice of my first station after dental school, but I didn't think that was their real objective.

The next day, I went in to see the captain. Appearing as contrite as I could, I asked, "About that transfer... What can I do?"

"It's what you *won't* do," he answered sternly. "You will no longer fraternize with the other lieutenants. You will no longer say anything to anyone that there is anything good about a career outside the Navy. And you will no longer work on recruits—we don't need you influencing those kids. Move all your instruments into the officers' clinic."

I immediately agreed. "And my transfer will be cancelled?"

"Already done. I was sure you'd figure things out." Before dismissing me, he added, "But watch yourself. I can write new orders at any time."

Although it's impossible for me to keep my mouth completely reined in, I kept a much lower profile from then on and was able to finish out my service in Orlando.

***

Jessica was born in the spring of 1984. Mother and daughter received excellent care in the Navy hospital, both were healthy, and Deborah and I had never been happier.

Our baby was the first grandchild for Deborah's parents, so of course they were thrilled, too. They had already flown down to visit us a number of times after our move to Orlando. Now they came more frequently, although never for very long. At the beginning of each visit, Deborah's mother would invariably say, "Guests are like fish. After three days, they start to smell." When three days had passed, her parents flew back home.

My parents were more subdued about the new granddaughter and visited less often. For one thing, my brother Anthony had already provided their first grandchild so the experience wasn't as novel. Also, my father rarely showed any emotion at all, and my mother was restrained in his presence. She always feared saying something that might anger him.

Although they came less frequently, my parents stayed longer than Deborah's, usually about a week. Since my father didn't fly, they made the long drive from New York in his four-door sedan. One of the suitcases they brought would always be filled with sausages, cheeses and other Italian delicacies that we couldn't get in Orlando.

It was funny in a way, because my father's friends packed the same luggage on their trips. Wiseguys from New York often spent periods of time in Florida and had provisions regularly driven down from Brooklyn. I'd heard that sometimes they would even have tanker trucks of New York City water sent down to be used in baking their bread.

There were never any conflicts during my parents' visits. My father would reorganize the garage and other things around the house, but we simply put them back the way we wanted after he left. And at least he didn't start any trash fires in the backyard, so none of my possessions went up in smoke.

***

Along with the joy of our first child came additional responsibilities. I would be leaving the Navy later that year and losing the regular paycheck that had been our main income. I now had to devote myself to preparing for an independent practice that could support a family of three.

Although I hadn't yet lined up the necessary funding, I began looking for a site where I could set up a dental office. I found a great location in Winter Park, less than ten minutes from our house, just off a major highway.

Dr. Gregory Samano was an osteopath with a thriving family practice. He already owned a medical complex of seven offices and had recently had an identical building constructed nearby. Dr. Samano wanted different kinds of medical care to be available, and he was looking for a dentist to be one of the tenants. I met with him, thought he was a great guy and loved his vision for the complex. I wanted to be part of it, but there was one problem: I still had several months of Navy service ahead of me and he couldn't hold the space for that long.

I had an idea for a solution and ran it past my friend Jerry, another lieutenant who intended to go into private practice. I proposed that we go into business together. By sharing the office condo, it would be more affordable for both of us, and since Jerry was due to leave the Navy in only a month or so we could take occupancy.

Jerry thought it was a good idea and the two of us went to view the site of the new complex. He liked it so much that he tried to stab me in the back. Without telling me, Jerry went to Dr. Samano and said he wanted the space for himself. When Dr. Samano asked, "What about Carl?" Jerry told him to forget about me. Jerry had enough money to set up the practice on his own and could cut me out of the space. "If that's how you do business," Dr. Samano replied, "I don't want you in my building. I like Carl, and I don't like you or what you're trying to do to him." Dr. Samano then called me and promised to hold the space until I was able to move in.

That was great news, but the space was only a shell at this point—and it wasn't going to be rent-free. I needed a bank loan for construction of the interior and to purchase equipment and furnishings. One hundred thousand dollars was the estimate I came up with to complete construction, set up the practice and carry me through the first few months. Unfortunately, my dreams exceeded my financial reality and the first two banks I approached turned me down.

Then I tried Coral Gables Savings and Loan, which occupied a unique circular building in downtown Orlando. I went into my appointment carrying a twelve-page letter that I'd written the night before. It wasn't a business plan—I didn't know how to write one of those—but more like an essay explaining why my practice would be successful.

A young loan officer took the time to read it and asked me a number of questions. I admitted to him that I had a mortgage on a house with no equity, car payments to make and student loans that I would soon need to begin repaying.

He considered all the information and said, "I've never seen anyone with your enthusiasm and commitment. Your financial numbers aren't what we would normally like to see, but you have me convinced. I'm going to take your application to the board and recommend that it be approved."

Coral Gables gave me a signature loan that allowed me to borrow up to one hundred thousand dollars as I needed it. Thanks to that loan officer who believed in me, I was able to proceed with building my dental office. And when it opened, that young man and his parents were among my first patients.

The Navy had been a great experience for me, and I will always be grateful for what it taught me and for the support it provided. It was a privilege to serve with some outstanding officers and practitioners. But professionally I had come to think of the service as a stepping-stone on my path forward. I only hoped that I wasn't going to be stepping off a cliff.

7. Margarita Drive

When our friends in New York and New Jersey saw that our Florida street address was Margarita Drive, they assumed that Deborah and I spent our days lounging by a pool, living out the lyrics to a Jimmy Buffet song. The truth was we had almost no leisure time. We had quite a few challenges facing us and it was an ongoing struggle to meet them.

One unexpected setback was the short duration of my separation from the Navy. My enlistment ended on a Friday in August, and I was scheduled to begin full-time work in Dr. Sanchez's office on Monday. Sunday afternoon, however, I suffered a broken jaw playing softball. Not knowing what to do, I called a captain at the base who was an oral surgeon. I explained that I had no insurance and asked his advice.

"Well..." he drawled. "Technically, we still own you. Report to the base at oh-seven-hundred tomorrow—in uniform."

He was correct that I was still bound to the Navy; my time wouldn't officially expire until Monday night. When you leave the service, you are put on "temporary active duty" for three days so that you have time to travel to your new destination.

I did as the captain instructed, and received a lot of ribbing from the other officers when I showed up in full uniform. The most frequent comment was, "Your private practice sure didn't last long!"

The captain telephoned Washington, spoke with an admiral, and made me an offer: "We can extend your duty for two months. You'll continue to work in the clinic, and the Navy will take care of your jaw." This was very generous and I was happy to accept.

I went back to work as before, full-time for the Navy Dental Corps and part-time with Dr. Sanchez. In addition, I was dealing with an architect and a general contractor to build the office suite I'd be leasing from Dr. Samano. All of the interior walls needed to be put in, along with the extensive electrical and plumbing services that were necessary for a dental office. If construction went according to schedule, I could open my practice in the spring.

Two weeks before the end of my extended duty, the captain called me into his office. "I've spoken to the admiral again," he said. "You are one of our brightest stars and we don't want to lose you."

I had no idea where he was going with this, but I was starting to have a flashback to the conversation that began similarly more than a year ago—the one that ended with a threat to send me to Okinawa. With such a short time remaining, I wondered, what could they threaten me with at this late date?

The captain went on, "You are aware that no one under the rank of captain supervises a Navy dental clinic?"

"Yes, sir."

"Well, the admiral is offering to make an exception for you. If you sign up for four more years, you and your family will spend that time in Hawaii. There's a clinic in Oahu, and you will be in charge of it. What do you say to four years in paradise?"

I was completely taken by surprise and didn't know what to say. I replied that I would give the proposal serious consideration. I knew that if I remained in the service I could also expect a promotion to Lieutenant Commander in a year or two. It was an attractive offer, and if it had been made a few months earlier I probably would have accepted on the spot.

After discussing it with Deborah, we decided to stick to our original plans. Construction on the office had already begun, and I had been paying for it with the bank loan; there was no way to cancel the project at this point. Besides, although I treasured my Navy experience, I didn't think it would be a long-term fit with my personality. I was about as suited to operating within military constraints as Hawkeye Pierce in *M*A*S*H*.

When I gave the captain my decision, he accepted it graciously and wished me well. I finished out my final two weeks and was off on my own!

***

In reality, I wasn't "on my own" at all. Although I was no longer part of an academic or military institution, my support system was unsurpassed—and I had been happily married to her for four years now.

Deborah had always been a hard worker and an independent thinker. During her school years, she held down jobs so that she could earn her own money and not have to ask her parents for anything. She was also very smart and knew how to plan ahead. While I tended to be impetuous, Deborah had more forethought. Fortunately, my enthusiasm and her planning skills meshed nicely and we made a great team.

Although Deborah had earned a master's degree in early childhood education from Fairleigh Dickinson, she didn't go into the teaching profession when we moved to Orlando. She had realized from the start that, once I opened my practice, I would need her to organize and coordinate the office. With that in mind, she set out to learn everything that she could about the operations of a dental practice. She worked as an office manager for several dentists in the area, mastering the details involved in running such an operation effectively.

In addition to gaining experience in office procedures, government regulations and the mass of paperwork that went along with any kind of medical practice, Deborah had the foresight to realize that we couldn't afford to hire full-time staff. So she went through a dental assisting program, as well as a radiology course, and became licensed to assist me with patients.

Deborah even surprised me by arranging for our first vacation since we'd been married. During my final summer in the Navy, I came home one day and Deborah told me to apply for a week's leave because we were going on a Caribbean cruise. She had already called Dr. Sanchez to tell him I wouldn't be coming in that week. My wife knew that if she'd asked me first, I would have objected to the cost. But she also knew that we badly needed a getaway and pointed out, "Once the practice opens, it will be years before we have another chance for a vacation."

Deborah was right on both counts. The cruise was exactly the relaxing break we needed after all the work we'd be doing. And it was our last one for some time thereafter.

***

Once I'd completed my extended Navy service, I was slated to work full-time for Dr. Sanchez while construction went on in my own facility. However, he feared that my practice could become competition for his own, and he wanted me to buy into his practice instead. He even presented me with papers that's he'd already had drawn up by his lawyers. I declined the partnership and proceeded with my plans.

Dr. Sanchez retaliated by firing me—and he didn't have the courtesy to do it in person. I learned that I'd been terminated when I arrived at work and saw my name crossed out on the schedule book. Dr. Sanchez later gave me a number of reasons, none of which were convincing. He wouldn't even let me finish my open cases—although by law he was required to—and demanded that I turn in my key. From what I gathered later, he was worried that some of his patients would follow me to my new practice. He calculated that by firing me he would cost me money and delay my chance to compete with him.

The loss of income from Dr. Sanchez was certainly a financial hit, but it didn't postpone my plans by a single day. In fact, it might have expedited matters. The hours I would have spent working for him I instead used to prepare my own practice.

Other than that one cruise, Deborah and I had lived frugally during my time in the Navy. We rarely went out to dinner and our hobbies were inexpensive ones. We had been able to put enough money in the bank that we could live off of our savings until the new practice opened.

While construction continued, I used my time to research how I could provide my future patients with the best possible care. I was already familiar with the equipment at the Naval Training Center and Dr. Sanchez's office; now, I visited a number of other dental practices in the area to determine the best equipment, instruments and materials. I also checked out the local laboratories which made crowns, bridges and dentures; I asked top dentists in the area which labs they used and inspected each facility that they recommended.

In addition, I made appointments with the top specialists in the area—periodontists, orthodontists, oral surgeons—to introduce myself and get a feel for how they dealt with patients. I would often have to refer my patients to such specialists and I wanted to be sure I would be putting them in good hands. There were two things I looked for in a specialist. One was communication: I wanted the other doctor to communicate with me about any treatment plan that was proposed for a patient of mine. The second consideration was a question: Whom would I want working on *my* teeth? Throughout my years of dentistry, before making recommendations to patients, I always asked myself, "What would I want done if it was my teeth?"

Our practice opened in April of 1985. The staff consisted of Deborah and myself, with Jessica occupying a playpen in the waiting room. Deborah had done a wonderful job on the interior decorating, I had made sure that the instruments and equipment were all first-rate, and the construction had gone exactly according to plan. Now all we needed were patients.

***

Although we started small, with only a single chair and one x-ray machine, all too often it was more than we needed. Deborah's appointment book had a lot of blank spaces, and for the first months of the practice she kept all of the patients' paperwork in a single shoebox. But on the upside, we were able to spend a lot of time playing with Jessica.

My first patient was a neighbor who lived across the street from us on Margarita Drive. When she paid, she included a dollar bill on which she'd written as a joke, "From your first victim." She was happy with my work and spread the word about me in our neighborhood.

Dr. Samano, who owned the medical complex, recommended me to his patients, and as I became more involved with the Greater Orlando Dental Society I began receiving referrals from other dentists. A pediatrician who lived near us recommended me to the parents of her patients, a few followed me from Dr. Sanchez's practice and others were retired military personnel who'd heard about me from my Navy friends.

One thing I did not do was advertise, or offer coupons or other gimmicks. I felt that the best way to become established for the long-term was by word-of-mouth from satisfied patients. If they believed that I cared about them and treated them the way I wanted to be treated, they would recommend me to their friends. It might be slower than advertising, but I wanted to base my practice strictly on the premise of quality care.

The first couple of years were pretty lean, but we managed to pay our bills and keep our home. Eventually, we had enough business to take on part-time staff and enough income to pay their salaries. Jessica also had more attention from patients who enjoyed holding her and playing with her in the waiting area.

***

I don't think anyone who's met me would conclude that I lacked self-confidence, but I actually did feel insecure about my skill set. You can be at the top of your class coming out of dental school, but that doesn't make you a top dentist. I knew that it required years of experience, diagnosing and treating an extensive range of dental problems, before a practitioner could be considered truly accomplished.

In order to compensate somewhat for my lack of experience, I undertook intensive studies in a number of disciplines. Having a light patient schedule when I began gave me time to travel and learn from some of the top authorities in their fields.

While I was in the Navy, I had already done some training in endodontics at the Walter Reed Army Medical Center in Washington. I now went to Dallas for an orthodontic program developed by Dr. Robert Gerety, one of the best teachers I've ever had. Deborah and I both flew to California to do a hands-on study with Dr. Robert Ibsen who invented porcelain veneers. Closer to home, I did an implant residency at the University of Miami and undertook a two-year full-mouth restoration program in Orlando.

I was eventually awarded a number of honors. I became a Master in the American Academy of Implant Prosthodontics, was elected to the Pierre Fauchard International Honor Society, and was named a Master in the International Congress of Implantology by Dr. Carl Misch himself, who is considered the father of implantology.

Although it felt great to be recognized by these societies and academies, there was a much more important result of my additional studies: I was confident that I could provide my patients with an expanded range of treatments and perform them capably.

***

Deborah continued to run the office until the day before our son Bryan was born in 1987. Here, too, she had planned ahead by hiring and training the person who would take her place at the front desk. With a toddler and an infant, she was leaving the practice to stay at home with the children.

The practice was now well enough established that we were sure we were going to make a success of it. We increasingly included leisure time in our schedule, although, as Deborah had predicted, long vacations were not possible. Our favorite family outing was to Disney's Magic Kingdom. Deborah had made a Minnie Mouse outfit for Jessica and I loved taking photos of her at the park. We also visited Epcot, which had opened after our move to Orlando; here, I liked to take photos with the sparkling Spaceship Earth geodesic dome as a backdrop.

With a growing family, our house on Margarita Drive was starting to seem a bit small and we began looking for another place to live. In 1989, we moved into a new home in Tuskawilla. The house had a swimming pool and there were excellent schools nearby for Jessica and Bryan.

Although we were excited about the move, Deborah and I were also sorry to be leaving our first house and the place where we had started our family. Most of the people who moved into the development had been young couples like us, just starting out. We had established close friendships with many of them, helped each other through difficult times and celebrated each other's successes. In a way, both the neighborhood and the residents had grown up together over the past five years.

Despite some sadness at what we were leaving behind, Deborah and I were comforted by the fact that we would be taking some great memories with us. We were also certain that there were more wonderful people and experiences in our future.

8. Shutterbug

On October 14, 1976, I was a working-class college student, feeling immensely lucky to be at Yankee Stadium for the final game of the American League championship series. To document the event, I had brought with me a little Kodak Instamatic, a simple point-and-shoot device one step above a Brownie box camera. I couldn't even imagine at that time that someday I would go on to take photographs of lions in Kenya, coral in the Great Barrier Reef, and snowy owls in Canada, using some of the most sophisticated equipment ever made.

My friend Warren, another R. A. in our dorm at Fairleigh Dickinson, told me he had a spare ticket for the playoff game and asked if I'd like to join him. For a Yankee fan like me, that was an easy question to answer! The Yankees hadn't won a pennant in twelve years, the championship series with Kansas City was tied at two games apiece, and tickets for the deciding game were being scalped at prices far beyond my subsistence budget.

I don't know how he got them, but Warren and I had great seats behind first base. It was a perfect vantage point for photography. Fortunately, I'd brought lots of film with me because I took photos of everything I could see—the crowd, the players, the scoreboard. I was like a little kid again, as excited as I'd been when Uncle Lloyd had brought me here to see my first big-league game in 1964.

Despite being a novice with the camera, I managed to get some nice action shots of Kansas City Royals stars

George Brett and John Mayberry. They both hit home runs, much to the dismay—and jeers—of the Stadium crowd. I also snapped photos of my favorite Yankees: Thurman Munson, Graig Nettles, Mickey Rivers and Roy White.

Incredibly, my Instamatic and I became eyewitness to history. With the game tied at six runs apiece, Yankees first baseman Chris Chambliss came to bat in the bottom of the ninth inning. He promptly hit the first pitch delivered to him over the right field wall. It was the first walk-off home run in a League Championship series and sent the New York Yankees to the World Series!

I took as many photos of Chambliss as I could, but he was soon lost in a crowd of jubilant fans who poured out of the stands and onto the field. Although Yankee Stadium only held about fifty-five thousand, it seemed that a hundred thousand fans were celebrating. Chambliss couldn't even complete his run around the basepaths because he was blocked by the swarming crowd. The umpires ultimately decided to count his run as having scored even though he never made it to home plate.

Warren and I were among those who had hopped the railings to join the celebration on the field. I continued to snap photographs. Rarely was there a scene of such widespread rejoicing, and I was eager to capture it on film.

Days later, when I received the developed prints from the lab, I was amazed at how intensely they enabled me to relive the joy that I'd felt during the game. When I showed the pictures to friends who hadn't been there, I could tell that the photos almost transported them to the ballpark and allowed them to share in the experience. I realized then that photography had a marvelous power to elicit emotional responses.

***

The following summer, together with a couple of friends, I went on a cross-country automobile trip before starting dental school. Our goal was to see as much of America as we could in twenty days, and of course I brought my Kodak.

We headed west on Interstate 80, the three of us crammed into a Pontiac Astre Hatchback. Since the car only had two seats, we rotated throughout the journey, one of us having to lie in back with our provisions and our clothes.

When we reached the Great Plains, we took a northerly route to visit Mount Rushmore, Yellowstone National Park and the Grand Tetons. These were spectacular sights and I tried my best to capture their majesty on film. In addition to the landscapes, I was awed by the wildlife. I had always loved animals, and took dozens of photos of the bison and the deer in Yellowstone.

Our westward leg of the journey ended in San Francisco. It was here that I witnessed one of the strangest scenes of the trip, but neglected to take any pictures of it. My friends and I walked into a pizza joint, and almost everyone was eating their pizzas with a knife and fork! We thought we'd encountered an alien culture or something. At one table, three young women about our age were holding their pizzas correctly so we went over and introduced ourselves. It turned out they were from Brooklyn. We spent a couple of days touring the city with them and they threw me a party for my twenty-second birthday.

Then we were off in our hatchback again, driving down the Pacific Coast Highway, allowing me to photograph the ocean and the beaches. At Hermosa Beach, we turned east for the return trip. We encountered very different scenes, now, as beautiful in their own way as the mountains and plains in the north. I took pictures of the Petrified Forest and Painted Desert in Arizona, the mesas of New Mexico and the canyons of Colorado, although I knew their subtleties of color and shading were beyond my ability to record on film.

When I got back from the trip, I looked over the pictures I'd taken and was again struck by the way photography could capture moments in time and preserve memories. I also realized that my rudimentary attempts could be vastly improved upon. I decided to buy a "real" camera and really learn the art.

**

Within a month of coming home, shortly before classes were to begin, I managed to scrape up three hundred dollars for a new 35 mm Canon AE-1 SLR camera. This model had come out the previous year and was fast becoming a favorite among amateur photographers. Unlike my point-and-shoot Instamatic, the AE-1 had all sorts of dials and dozens of different settings, none of which I understood. It could also accommodate different lenses, but this wasn't a problem since I couldn't afford any additional lenses.

When the semester started, our class of dental students had to set up a number of committees to handle various responsibilities. One of these was to produce the yearbook that would be published when we graduated in four years. I was named head of the photography committee, with several other students under me. In addition to providing photos for the yearbook, we had to document dental procedures and do intraoral photography, which is an important way for dentists to record a patient's condition and treatment.

Although I had a full load of academic courses, I also applied myself to learning the operation of my new camera. I'm not the type to simply follow a manual, so I undertook an extensive trial-and-error approach. I experimented with various settings, learned about apertures and focal lengths, and kept notes on each configuration and the images that resulted.

Came October, I was in Yankee Stadium again, this time for the World Series against the Dodgers. In the final game, Reggie Jackson hit three home runs to win it for New York and I got some spectacular photos. With my new camera, the images were much more captivating than the ones I had produced only a year earlier.

Many of my early efforts were directed toward sports photography. I was fascinated by the idea of freezing time in an action shot. A year after Jackson's heroics, I photographed the 1978 World Series, another victory over the Dodgers, and again saw significant improvement in the results.

Among the photos I sadly never got to see were some that I took of Yankee captain Thurman Munson in July, 1979. He had accommodated me by posing a few times, and

I was sure I'd gotten some excellent shots. A week after I sent the negatives to a lab, Munson was tragically killed in a plane crash. When my prints failed to arrive, I telephoned the lab and they claimed to have lost my film. I'll always remember the last time I'd seen Munson play, but I sure wish I had those images.

When I met Deborah, I began to teach myself portrait photography. In addition to camera settings and composition, lighting and backdrops were important considerations. As I experimented with these, Deborah was always patient and obliging. She was also a beautiful model, so even when I made mistakes it was impossible for the photograph to look bad!

At the end of my last year in dental school, my class needed to have our picture taken for the yearbook and that responsibility fell to me. We were all somewhat giddy from having successfully completed our studies and we were feeling cocky about our future careers. So I suggested that we stage our class photo in a different venue from the usual. When my classmates heard what I had in mind, they loved the idea and we made the arrangements.

The Class of 1981 at Fairleigh Dickinson's College of Dental Medicine didn't have its picture taken on campus. Instead, our photo was shot at a local Mercedes dealership with all of us standing around my dream car: a 450 SL convertible.

***

Some of the best guidance I received in photography came after our move to Florida when Deborah's parents would visit. Her dad Henry was a technical genius and an accomplished photographer. He understood the physics of optical systems and knew how to use all the available accessories to optimize a picture.

When he was in Orlando, Henry and I always went out together to take photos, usually of birds and nature. One of our favorite places was Gatorland, which had been a local attraction since before I was born. While children came to the park eager to see the enormous alligators and crocodiles, Henry and I were primarily interested in the rookery. We took photographs of wood storks, snowy egrets, blue herons and red-shouldered hawks. When Seaworld's Discovery Cove opened, we spent time in its free-flight aviary, which housed hundreds of tropical and exotic birds. I quickly learned that taking a photo of a mountain or a portrait of Deborah was a lot easier than trying to capture an osprey taking off in flight! With instruction from Henry, though, I began to learn the subtleties involved in wildlife photography and started to produce some decent images.

Henry was even proficient in medium format photography. This was usually the domain of professionals, both because of the cost of the apparatus and the technical ability needed to employ it effectively. Among other things, the camera used a much larger-sized film than 35 mm and could take in more detail.

Medium format was far beyond me, so I continued to try to master 35 millimeter. Here, too, I relied on Henry's advice regarding my equipment. His everyday camera was a

Nikon and he convinced me to make the switch from Canon because he felt Nikon had better lenses. The Canon versus Nikon debate has raged for decades among photographers; for me, it was enough that Henry came down on the Nikon side.

Henry also recommended a number of additional lenses and other accessories, but I couldn't afford them. I was on a Navy paycheck and trying to save up to start a dental practice. He also helped me here: Whenever my birthday came around, a new lens or piece of equipment would show up in the mail as a present from Henry.

Those photography outings were among my fondest experiences during the first years we lived in Orlando. I was able to explore scenic Florida, capture some of its grandeur on film and develop a bond with my father-in-law.

***

For a baseball fan, Florida is one of the best places on earth to live. Its weather has always been conducive to the game and the sport has thrived. There are numerous minor league teams that play throughout the summer, and many of the major league clubs, including the Yankees and the Dodgers, established their spring training camps in the Sunshine State.

Tinker Field, in downtown Orlando, had been home to professional baseball since the 1920s and some of the game's best players, from Babe Ruth to Hank Aaron, played there. Near the Disney parks, in Kissimmee, was the Astros' minor league club. In Daytona Beach and Lakeland were two more teams.

A great feature of these ballparks is that they are much smaller than major league stadiums. They allow greater proximity to the field and the players, and the atmosphere is much more casual. It's easy to speak with the players and the rules aren't as strict. Being able to get close is an advantage in photography, and I made the most of it. In addition to taking action shots during games, I sought to get photos of individual players during warmups. Many of them, especially the young ones just beginning their careers, were willing to pose briefly so that I could take portraits, and I began to acquire a substantial collection.

With the NBA expanding in 1989, Central Florida had a new professional basketball team, the Orlando Magic, and I had another sports venue to visit. During their early years, I attended quite a few games, frequently taking Jessica along with me. The seating capacity of the Orlando Arena was about that of a minor league ballpark, so fans were close to the players and the action.

I expanded my sports photography efforts to include basketball. It took a lot of trial and error, but I enjoyed the challenge of adapting to an indoor setting, artificial lighting and constant movement. Jessica and I would typically arrive early, and we were allowed to walk around right next to the court as the players warmed up. I took numerous photos of the Magic players as well as those on the visiting clubs.

As with my baseball photos, I soon built up a collection of basketball prints and wanted to get some of them autographed. I would bring a pair of prints of each image and offer one to the player. I introduced myself, telling them that I was a dentist in Winter Park and wanted to display the photos in my office for my patients to see and enjoy. I also asked the players to inscribe the prints for me so they knew the photos really were for my personal use. I wasn't a dealer and have never sold any autograph I've been given.

The new club encouraged the team to help build a fan base by maintaining good relations with the public, and I found the players to be very accommodating and friendly. Even the Magic's top stars, like Nick Anderson and Penny Hardaway, were terrific about signing. Understandably, few of them were willing to take on the challenge of my last name, though, so the photos were almost always signed "To Dr. B." and that's what the players and staff began to call me.

Shaquille O'Neal joined the team as a rookie in 1992. He was a great guy who was also happy to sign. I later got to know him fairly well. Shaq was one of Jessica's favorites; he was over seven foot tall and she thought of him as a gentle giant.

Not only did the players give me autographs, but their reactions to the photos provided some of my best feedback. Sometimes the players would initiate conversations with me, checking to see if I'd taken any new pictures of them that they could have. If my images were bad, they wouldn't have wanted them—everybody wants to look good in a photo—so I interpreted their interest in getting more prints to mean that I was becoming proficient with my photography.

***

In 1993, Florida was awarded its first major league baseball franchise, the Miami-based Marlins. One day that summer, I was showing some photos to my friend Rick Susi, who had recently moved to Florida from Sharpsville, Pennsylvania. Sharpsville is in the western part of the state, and Rick was a devoted fan of every Pittsburgh professional sports team. The Pirates were scheduled to face the Marlins in a series, and we thought it might be a nice outing to drive to Miami and watch them play. Then I had an idea: I had photos of several Pirates players in my collection, and I decided we should try to get them signed.

I suggested to Rick, "Let's stay at the same hotel as the Pirates and see if they'll sign some pictures."

"Impossible," he said. "They never reveal where they're staying."

As usual, I took "impossible" as a challenge and went about proving Rick wrong. I got a list of Miami hotels and began making phone calls. "Could you connect me to Jim Leyland, please?" I'd say, asking for the Pirates manager. After each "no," I'd move on to the next hotel on the list. Finally, a receptionist answered, "Certainly. One moment please."

Now I was at a loss for words—a rare occurrence. I had thought that asking for the team's manager was simply a clever way of discovering the correct hotel. I hadn't considered what I would say if I was actually put through to him.

"Leyland here," a gruff voice said. "Who's this?"

"Uh... I just called to wish you good luck against the Marlins. Have a nice day!" And I hung up.

Now that we'd identified our destination, Rick and I drove down to Miami with our families. I brought with me two enlarged prints of each Pirate photo that I wanted signed. Soon after we checked into the hotel, Rick and I began prowling the public areas looking for the ballplayers. We found almost the entire Pittsburgh Pirates team hanging around the swimming pool.

I went back to the room, grabbed my stack of photos and headed out to the pool. When I approached a player whose photo I had, I'd hold it up for him to see. Typically, he'd notice and come over to me to look at it more closely. If it appeared that he liked it, I'd tell him, "I'd like to give this to you, if you want it. And if you don't mind, could you sign this copy for me?" I always had two prints of the photos on hand and would offer one to the player as a gift.

The first to sign was Tim Wakefield, a young knuckleballer who would go on to have a long and successful career with the Boston Red Sox. We found all of the players to be friendly and courteous. I gave away a number of photos to them, and they in turn autographed prints for me. Then Rick and I left them alone so that we wouldn't be intrusive.

When we attended Pittsburgh's series with Miami, we discovered that our brief interactions with the players somehow made the games a richer experience. There was more of a personal connection, and the signed photos were a wonderful way to preserve the memories of those encounters.

***

Although I enjoyed sporting events and meeting athletes, I began to devote more of my time to wildlife photography. The unpredictability of the weather, the environment and the subjects made capturing Florida's animals on film especially difficult. It required the technical skills to adjust camera settings quickly, an artistic eye for composing the shots and a whole lot of luck in finding interesting animals within camera range.

I've learned that luck most often results from hard work and preparation. Since my main interest was birds, I began studying the various species and became familiar with their nesting habits and migration routes. I tracked which species was most likely to be in a particular location at a particular time of year, then sought them out. I kept notes of each outing and discovered several places that almost always provided productive sessions. Among my favorite destinations for bird photography were Merritt Island Wildlife Refuge and Lake Apopka Wildlife Drive

Over the years, I took thousands of photographs—sporting events, portraits, landscapes and wildlife—but I never lost the sense of wonder that I'd felt when I saw the first images from my little Instamatic. I still marveled at how a photograph could freeze a moment in time and transport you back so that it could be relived and savored again and again. Whether a World Series home run celebration, a bald eagle in flight or a child's birthday party, there is magic in the way photographic images can bring memories to life.

9. Good Sports

When I was growing up in Brooklyn in the 1950s and '60s, major league baseball players were mythic figures to me. Their images were immortalized on baseball cards, their feats were recorded in bold headlines on the back pages of the *Daily News* and their names were used like magic incantations during stickball games—a boy stepping up to hit might announce, "It's Mickey Mantle coming to the plate!" as if invoking the Mick's name would guarantee a home run.

I never expected to see a big-league ballplayer in person other than from a seat in the bleachers. They were too remote, I believed, and didn't mingle with us mortals. Years later I had the pleasure of meeting quite a few of them, as well as stars from other sports, and was impressed by how unaffected most of them really were. I was also struck by the fact that many of those encounters came about in completely unexpected ways.

***

While I was in the Navy, I had developed an interest in coins and began a small collection of Morgan silver dollars. I became friends with Roger Bryan, president of the state numismatic society, whom I'd met at some coin shows in Orlando. In 1984, my last year in the service, Roger invited me to his home in Gainesville. He had received a bag of Morgan dollars from Nevada and thought I'd be interested in looking through them.

I drove up to Roger's place, a well-maintained house on the outskirts of the city, and he showed me where he kept his coins. It was a walk-in safe, the size of a small bedroom, outfitted with shelves and drawers. I saw that in addition to coins he had a variety of other collectibles, including Lionel trains and sports memorabilia.

Roger noticed me gawking at his autographed Yankees items. "You a Yankee fan?" he asked.

"Big time," I said. "How did you get all this?"

"Roger Maris is a friend of mine," he answered matter-of-factly. I must have appeared a bit skeptical. For a few years, the duo of Mantle and Maris, dubbed "The M&M Boys," were the home run kings of baseball. I didn't imagine either of them having friends who were ordinary people. "He lives right next door," Roger added. This, too, seemed unlikely. Surely a legend like Roger Maris lived in a mansion someplace, not in such a modest neighborhood as this one. But I tried not to betray my doubts to my host.

As I began examining the coins, Roger left me alone to make a phone call. I became absorbed in scrutinizing Morgan silver dollars, looking for the scarce Carson City mint marks.

About ten minutes later, to my complete astonishment, Roger Maris walked in. He looked in good enough shape to step into the batter's box at Yankee Stadium, and his hair was still styled in the trademark crewcut that he'd sported during his playing days.

Roger Bryan made the introductions and we sat around the kitchen table, talking baseball over cups of coffee. Maris turned out to be a soft-spoken and humble man, and I was quickly at ease with him. We talked about the current Yankee club, and Maris said he thought George Steinbrenner would do whatever it took to build a winning team.

Of course, I had to ask him about the historic 1961 season. The Yankees were the only team New Yorkers could root for at the time, with the Dodgers and Giants having moved to California and the Mets not yet in existence. And the big contest all year long was between the two Yankees sluggers, Mickey Mantle and Roger Maris, as they each made a run at Babe Ruth's single season home run record. The media coverage was intense and it was a daily topic of conversation from spring through fall. People didn't ask each other for updates on the Bay of Pigs invasion or construction of the Berlin Wall; they wanted to know whether Mantle or Maris hit a home run that day.

"That was a rough year," Maris said. "New York can be a hostile environment." He was from North Dakota. "It seemed everybody was against me, and I could never figure out what I did to make them hate me."

"Nobody I knew hated you," I said. "We all thought you were great.

"Thank you. You and your friends were in the minority though. Most people seemed to believe I was hurting baseball just by trying to do my job." He shook his head as if still trying to fathom the way he'd been treated.

Although I was too young to be aware of it at the time, I later learned how much resistance there had been to Maris's quest for the home run crown. Babe Ruth's record was considered sacred, especially by New Yorkers, and if anyone was to break it the only acceptable player to do so was fan favorite Mickey Mantle. When Maris hit his sixty-first homer to break Ruth's record on the last day of the season, the baseball commissioner tried to diminish his accomplishment. He said that the record books should put an asterisk next to Maris's total since Ruth had established the mark in fewer games.

"The newspapers were brutal," Maris went on sadly. "They cooked up a feud between Mickey and me which never existed—we always cheered each other on. I got so many death threats, the Yankees hired a police detective to follow me around wherever I went. My hair was even falling out from the stress." He shrugged. "All I was trying to do was play the best that I could and help my team win ballgames. I never understood what I did that was so wrong."

I could tell that after more than twenty years he was still hurting from the ordeal. To change the topic, I asked how he'd come to be living in Gainesville.

"I own a beer distributorship with my brother," he said. "After the Yankees traded me, I played my last couple of years with the St. Louis Cardinals. Gussie Busch owned both the Cards and Anheuser-Busch brewing. He set me up in the beer business when I left baseball." He smiled. "Gainesville is a lot friendlier than New York. I coach baseball for one of the high schools and nobody's ever threatened to kill me because of a game." Maris seemed to be growing tired at this point and excused himself to return home.

A week later, a dozen autographed baseballs unexpectedly arrived at my house, along with a note from Roger Maris. He'd inscribed one of the balls to me and asked me to give the others to friends. That was the first autographed baseball I ever received and it remains a cherished possession.

I was unaware at the time, and he hadn't said anything about it, but when I met him Maris had been battling non-Hodgkins lymphoma. He succumbed to the disease a year later at the age of fifty-one. I was among the millions of fans who mourned the loss of a boyhood hero who was more beloved than he realized.

***

In the late 1980s, one of my favorite places to visit was Boardwalk and Baseball, a dual-attraction theme park about forty miles south of Orlando. The Boardwalk section was designed to provide the atmosphere of a small-scale Coney Island or Atlantic City, with rides, shows and games. The Baseball side included batting cages and pitching mounds where guests could test their skills, as well as exhibits from the Baseball Hall of Fame. A new ballpark had also been built on the site, which became the spring training home of the Kansas City Royals. The amusement park only survived a few years, unable to compete with Disney, but baseball games continued and I went there often to take photographs.

The Boston Red Sox had played a memorable World Series against the Mets in 1986 and were among the first teams scheduled to play exhibition games at Boardwalk and Baseball the following spring. Of course, I went there with my camera and took dozens of photos of Boston stars like

Wade Boggs, Roger Clemons, Jim Rice and Dwight Evans. I got some particularly good shots of Boggs, who had just won his third batting championship.

A few years later, there was a televised auction to raise money for a Florida sports museum. One of the items offered was a day of fishing with Wade Boggs on Lochloosa Lake, near Gainesville, where his family owned the cleverly-named Finway Fish Camp. I placed a bid I hoped would be high enough to win. Not only would I enjoy spending a day with baseball's premier hitter, but I could ask him to sign some of the photos I'd taken of him at Boardwalk and Baseball.

I won the auction, sent in my check and received a very nice letter from Winfield Boggs, Wade's father, who ran the camp. He informed me that our outing would be scheduled during the off-season. I looked forward to the occasion, but when baseball season was over I was enrolled in an intensive dental course on full-mouth restoration. Photography and sports were passions of mine, but my priority was dentistry. I had a professional obligation to my patients and was committed to the course. Reluctantly, I gave up the day of fishing with Wade Boggs.

When I told the senior Mr. Boggs that I wouldn't be able to accept my prize, he asked if there was anything else I might want, such as autographs. I told him I would like to attend one of the Red Sox spring training games and see if Wade would sign the photos I'd taken of him. Mr. Boggs assured me this would be no problem, except that Wade was no longer with the Red Sox. He had just signed with the Yankees and I would have to travel to their facility in Fort

Lauderdale. I was grateful for the offer and looked forward to the spring.

In March of 1993, Jessica and I drove the three-plus hours to venerable Fort Lauderdale Stadium, which had been the Yankees spring training home for thirty years. Since Deborah was teaching at this time, she stayed home with Bryan. When Jessica and I arrived at the ballpark, we found that Boggs had left us passes at the ticket window and we went inside. Before taking our seats, I spotted him near the dugout. As a Yankee fan, I was happy to see him in pinstripes!

I went over to the rail and called out to Boggs that I was Dr. B. He immediately came over and we shook hands. Boggs was very cordial but appeared a bit troubled. "I'm really sorry, man," he said. "I thought I could get you access to the field and the clubhouse, but I can't. With the Red Sox it would have been no problem, but Steinbrenner has more rules than the I.R.S." Yankees owner George Steinbrenner had just resumed running the ballclub after a two-year suspension for violating a few rules himself.

I didn't blame Boggs, but my disappointment must have been evident. "Tell you what," he said, "Let me get you a signed ball now and I'll meet you after the game and sign anything you like." He went into the dugout and passed a baseball down the line. Not only were there active players on the bench, but some Yankee legends, too. When he gave me the ball, I saw the autographs of Hall-of-Famers Yogi Berra and Whitey Ford along with current stars like pitcher Jim Abbott and catcher Mike Stanley.

After the game, I met Boggs outside the players' gate as he'd suggested. He was generous with his time and we talked baseball for quite a while as he signed the photos from Boardwalk and Baseball along with some bats and balls.

Throughout the rest of Wade Boggs' Hall of Fame career, I often saw him at spring training camp, at local Yankees events and at Tropicana Field in Tampa. He would usually take a few minutes to chat with me and autograph whatever items I had. He even signed a little cookbook of his titled "Fowl Tips"—Boggs had become known as "Chicken Man" because he ate chicken every day, and after he won his first batting title he published some of his favorite recipes.

The best photo I ever took of Wade Boggs was at Game Six of the 1996 World Series against the Braves. I was in the upper mezzanine, and when the Yankees won the game to take their first title in eighteen years, the New York crowd went wild with excitement. It reminded me of the crazy scene I'd been part of in the 1976 playoffs. Mounted police patrolled the playing field, though, and fans couldn't storm it as they had in '76. Suddenly, a jubilant Wade Boggs hopped onto the back of one of the horses and I got a great shot of him riding around Yankee Stadium. The next spring I gave him a copy of the photo and he signed one for me.

There was only one item that Boggs refused to sign for me and it was from that same World Series. After the series, he had given one of his game-used bats to heavyweight boxing champion Evander Holyfield and inscribed it, "From one world champ to another." For some reason, Holyfield didn't keep the bat and it ended up in an auction. When I saw the listing, I submitted a bid and came away the winner.

Later, I showed it to Boggs at an autograph session. He was furious that Holyfield hadn't kept his gift and wouldn't sign the bat again.

Wade Boggs was one the major league ballplayers I came to know best, and I'm grateful for the time he spent with me. His approachability also eased my introduction to some of the other players; they saw me speaking with him and accepted me as something of a regular around the club.

***

Early in 1996, I was on a flight from Phoenix to Orlando, having witnessed Dallas beat the Pittsburgh Steelers in the Super Bowl. As I tend to do, I struck up a conversation with the passenger seated next to me, and mentioned that I'd been to the game.

"You a football fan?" he asked. He was big guy, about six-three, and looked like he could have played the sport.

"No, not really." I had only gone because a patient had given me a ticket and I thought it might be an interesting experience. "I like baseball."

"So do I. You have a favorite team?"

"The Yankees," I replied, as if no other answer was possible.

We continued to talk throughout the flight, with me doing most of it. I don't think my travel companion ever told me his last name or what he did for a living.

A few days after I returned to work, my office manager announced, "There's a John Sittig on the phone."

"Who's that?" I asked.

"He says he was on a flight with you last weekend."

I got on the line, and John said, "Carl, you really made my flight enjoyable and I want to do something to thank you." I told him that wasn't necessary, but he went on, "Legends Field has just opened and I want to give you and your family tickets for a game." Legends Field was the new spring training home of the Yankees in Tampa. Costing thirty million dollars, it was the largest spring training park in Florida and a state-of-the-art facility.

I again told John it wasn't necessary but was happy to accept. A couple of days later, I received the tickets in the mail, and on Saturday our family drove to Tampa for the ballgame.

As usual, I arrived well before game time so that I might wander around and take photographs. The envelope John had sent me included a parking pass, but no information on where I was supposed to park. I pulled up to an attendant and asked where I should go.

"You have this pass, and you don't know where to go?" he answered.

"If I knew, I wouldn't be asking." It was a brand new ballpark; how would anyone be familiar with it yet?

The grumpy attendant pointed to a small lot adjacent to the stadium. "Take any spot you want except number One."

"Why? Whose is that?"

"Mr. Steinbrenner's."

I pulled into spot number Two. We were dressed casually for a ballgame in warm Florida weather and carried a cooler. Our tickets didn't have any numbers or prices on them, so I didn't know where our seats were located. I found an usher and asked for directions.

Having apparently graduated from the same hospitality school as the parking lot attendant, he growled, "You don't know?" When I again said that if I knew I wouldn't be asking, he said, "What's in the cooler?"

"Sodas and sandwiches."

"Take it back to your car, then I'll tell you where to go."

"We can't bring a cooler in?"

"You can, but you won't want to."

I returned the cooler to the car and when I came back, the attendant made a phone call. The door of a nearby elevator opened and a man in a tuxedo stepped out. "This way, please," he politely invited us. A *tuxedo*? At a ballgame? I wondered who John Sittig was and what we were heading into.

We stepped off the elevator and were ushered onto the plush carpet of Luxury Suite Number Two. "Luxury" was certainly the right word for it! Not only were the furnishings exquisite, but there were platters of shrimp, lobster and all sorts of gourmet foods. An array of beverages was on a counter and a server was standing by.

Bryan, eight years old, did a quick run around the suite and came back to ask in awe, "Is all this because Daddy is a dentist?"

"No," Deborah answered. "It's because Daddy has a big mouth and talks to strangers on planes."

It turned out that John Sittig was an executive with Coopers & Lybrand, one of oldest accounting firms in the country, and did the accounting for the New York Yankees.

This was the company's suite and we were his guests. I sure opened my big mouth to the right person!

When batting practice began, I asked if we had to stay in the suite and was told that our pass allowed us to go anyplace in the ballpark. Deborah and Jessica decided to relax on a couch with plates of hors d'oeuvres while I grabbed my camera and went down toward the field with Bryan.

Legends Field had been specifically designed for the Yankees, first-class in every way. Not only was it the only spring training park with luxury suites, but the field itself had the same dimensions at Yankee Stadium in the Bronx. Even the style was similar, with a scalloped white frieze around the grandstand.

I'd taken a few photos of Derek Jeter in the batting cage when I noticed that Bryan was no longer standing next to me. He was an energetic boy and we were always having to track him down. I spotted him standing in the press area next to the Yankees dugout. I called to get his attention, but he seemed very content with his spot and not inclined to leave it. The game hadn't even started, and I worried that we were going to be thrown out before it began.

Bryan had also caught the eye of a Yankee legend. Reggie Jackson was walking by and spotted my son in the press circle. "Hey kid," he called and tossed Bryan a baseball.

I shouted to Bryan, "That's Mr. October!"

My son had no idea who Reggie Jackson was, but he liked his new baseball. "Thanks, Mr. October!" he said as he ran away with the ball.

I cupped my hands around my mouth and yelled for Bryan to ask Jackson if he would sign the ball, but my son had already scampered out of earshot. I gave up on photography for a while, tracked down Bryan and brought him back to the suite. John Sittig had arrived, along with other members of his firm. We made the introductions and settled down to watch the ballgame.

Until now, Luxury Suite Number One, about three times the size of ours, had been empty. Suddenly George Steinbrenner arrived with his entourage. I saw "The Boss" but was not going to risk approaching the often irascible owner for an autograph or anything. I didn't want John to regret having invited us.

Bryan had no such qualms. Holding his baseball, he ran into the adjacent box where Steinbrenner was surveying his new ballpark. "Who are you?" Bryan asked him.

The Yankee boss looked around. "George Steinbrenner. And where did you come from?"

Bryan pointed at our suite. "I'm with those people." Everyone in our box froze with fear at what Steinbrenner's reaction would be. My son held out the ball. "Would you sign my baseball?"

"I'd be happy to." Steinbrenner signed, and I hoped Bryan would come back to our box without further incident.

Then Bryan noticed the woman sitting next to Steinbrenner. "Who are you?" he asked her.

"Joan Steinbrenner," she said. It was the Boss's wife.

"Would you sign my ball?"

"Oh, you don't want my autograph." The others in the suite coaxed her into signing the baseball, probably hoping it would make the little boy leave sooner.

Bryan immediately came back to our box with his prize and I tucked it away for safe keeping. As I did, somebody inside Suite Number One quietly closed the connecting door between the two boxes.

My son still has that prized baseball, a memento of a remarkable experience. And it all came about because I talk to strangers on planes.

***

I believe that photographs are meant to be shared. They allow another person to experience a feeling or view a scene that they hadn't been able to witness firsthand. One of the ways I liked to share my photos is by simply giving them away.

Before digital photography, I would get four-by-six prints developed from all the film I had shot, then choose the ones I wanted to keep and enlarge. That left me with a lot of extra prints.

Since I had season tickets to the Orlando Magic basketball games, I became a familiar figure, taking photos and talking with the players and staff. I got to know a couple of the ushers who worked day jobs at a downtown middle school. They told me most of the students were ardent basketball fans, so I gave them hundreds of prints, featuring Michael Jordan, Shaquille O'Neal, Karl Malone, Patrick Ewing, Scottie Pippen and many other NBA stars, that they could distribute to the kids.

One of my other giveaways was to a complete stranger. I had taken a spectacular photo of Penny Hardaway and Shaq facing off against each other in a game. This was in 1997, and it was O'Neal's first appearance back at the Arena since he'd gone to the Lakers. I enlarged the print, and when I examined it I noticed that in the background between the players a man was hugging a boy I assumed to be his son. Their expressions were of complete joy, and the fact that they were framed by Hardaway and O'Neal gave the image terrific composition.

The man and boy had been seated in an area usually occupied by season ticket holders so I thought I'd keep an eye out for them. At the next game, I went to the spot where I'd snapped the photo and looked across the court toward the section that appeared in the print. There was the same man, who resembled Jay Leno with less of a jaw, but he was unaccompanied this time.

I walked over to him and handed him the enlarged print. "I thought you might like this," I said.

He took it from me and immediately smiled when he saw it. "That's my son Michael and me. I love it! How much do you want?"

"I don't want anything. It's a gift. If somebody took a photo like that of me with my son, I know I'd enjoy having a copy, so I thought you would too." That's how I determined a lot of what I did in life; I simply tried to treat others the way I would want to be treated.

The man looked surprised, thanked me, and I went back to my regular seat. He then asked one of the ushers who I was, and learned that I was "Dr. B." and a regular photographer at the Arena.

A couple of games later, the man came over to where I was sitting with Rick Susi, the same friend who had joined me on that trip to Miami to see the Pittsburgh Pirates. He introduced himself as Joe Sardano and we started talking sports. He asked if I was a baseball fan.

"Fuggedaboutit," I said in the Brooklyn affirmative. "In fact, Rick and I are going to New York in two weeks to see the Yankees play the Montreal Expos."

"I'm from Montreal!" Sardano said. He told us he'd had a tryout with the Montreal Canadiens hockey team years earlier. "I'm a big Expos fan."

Without thinking, I said, "Maybe you should come with us."

"I'd love to." He handed me his business card. "Call my secretary and tell her to make the same arrangements for me that you're making."

Sardano returned to his regular seat and Rick and I looked at the business card. Joe Sardano was the CEO of General Electric's Medical Systems.

"What did you just do?" Rick asked me. "This guy probably flies in private jets and stays at four-star hotels. I don't think he's going to want to duplicate our arrangements."

I walked over to Sardano to confess the low-budget arrangements Rick and I typically made. "I don't think the way Rick and I travel is what you're used to," I said. "We fly into Newark, my father picks us up and we stay at my parents' little townhome in New Jersey. We have dinner at our favorite Italian restaurant in Bayonne and I borrow my father's car to drive to the game. Nothing fancy."

Sardano looked at me and said, "That sounds like a really good time." He was in.

I went back to tell Rick that Sardano would be joining us. "What are you going to tell your father?" he asked. I hadn't considered that, and it could be an obstacle.

When I telephoned to tell my father there would be another houseguest, he squawked, "What the hell are you doin' bringin' strangers into my home?"

I told him Joe Sardano was a nice guy and wouldn't be any trouble. "And he's Italian," I added.

"Those are the worst kind," my father said.

Joe Sardano actually fit right in with us, and even my father seemed to like him. With their children all grown, my parents now lived in a small two-bedroom townhome in Hightstown, New Jersey. Rick and Joe shared the spare bedroom and I slept on the couch. We had dinner at Luciano's in Bayonne and then went to Yankee Stadium for the game.

We arrived early and headed to our box seats near the Montreal dugout. Gary Carter, the retired catcher and future Hall-of-Famer, was walking past and Joe Sardano called to him, "Hey, California Kid!"

Carter looked up in recognition. "Joe! How are you doing?" He waved to him. "Come on down! Bring your friends!"

I asked Joe, "You know him?"

"Oh yeah, ever since he was with the Expos." Carter had had a stellar career with Montreal before going to the Mets and was a fan favorite in both cities.

We went onto the field, Carter cheerfully posed for photos and signed some autographs, and we all talked and joked around. The first pitch hadn't been thrown yet, and it was already one of the most enjoyable games I'd been to!

I saw Gary Carter several times over the years and he always remembered me. Once he was appearing at a card show in Orlando and I brought Deborah and Jessica along to see him. He called to me, "Hey Dr. B!" We talked for a while, and he again posed for photos and signed some autographs. He was one of the most engaging and friendly major leaguers I had come to know. Sadly, he died of brain cancer at age fifty-seven.

My friendship with Joe Sardano continued. At first, he had been a stranger in the background of a photograph. But because I wanted to share that image with him, I acquired a lifelong friend.

***

I had been a regular at Orlando Magic games for more than ten years and was familiar to the staff and players. But it wasn't until a newcomer joined the club that I was asked to be the team's official dentist.

Doc Rivers had been an all-star point guard for a number of teams, including the New York Knicks. His playing career over, he was hired as the new head coach of the Orlando Magic for the 1999-2000 season. Before moving to Orlando, he asked his dentist in New York to recommend one in central Florida. I was the one he suggested. Rivers asked some other dentists for recommendations and my name was the one he kept hearing.

Rivers thus became my patient and I treated him soon after his arrival in Florida. He was so pleased with my work that he asked if I would be the Magic's team dentist. There was no pay, other than for specific treatments I provided, but I would be given credentials and an all-access pass. I already had season tickets, so free admission didn't help me, but I liked the idea of helping out a team I'd enjoyed watching for years and I accepted.

Although basketball is often considered a noncontact sport, the players take a lot of hits. One of the most common is when a mouthful of teeth gets in the way of a swinging elbow. During games, I would sometimes have to take a player into the locker room to examine the damage and, if possible, patch him up well enough to go back in the game. More extensive restoration and treatment would then be done in my office. Among the players I treated were Dwight Howard, Tracy McGrady and Turkish star Hedo Turkoglu.

Doc Rivers did such a great job with the Magic that in his first season he was named the NBA's Coach of the Year. He spent three more years with Orlando, and I continued to serve as the team's dentist for another decade after that.

Several of the players remained patients of mine after their careers were over. I believe they felt I provided them with quality care, and I know that they loved seeing the photos I'd taken of them over the years displayed on my office walls.

***

One of the first professional athletes to become a patient of mine was neither a baseball player nor a basketball player. It was Greg Sacks, a champion NASCAR driver, and my work with him led me to my first movie set.

Greg was one of the top stock car drivers in the 1980s, winning the Firecracker 400 at Daytona International Speedway in 1985, the same year that I opened my practice. He lived in central Florida and began coming to me for his dental care.

When the Tom Cruise movie *Days of Thunder* was being filmed, Paramount Pictures needed a professional to do the actual driving. Greg Sacks was hired to double for Cruise in the racing scenes as well as provide additional action footage on the track. Producers felt that there was one problem with Greg, though: His lower teeth were slightly crooked—not much, but enough to be noticeable on a movie screen. The picture's medical director wanted to send Greg to the studio dentist, but he refused. "Nobody touches my teeth except Dr. B," Greg told them.

"Who's that?"

"Dr. Bilancione in Winter Park. He's my personal dentist."

The medical director agreed to let Greg come to me for the procedure, and I was able to do some bonding that produced excellent results. The producers liked my work so much that when one of the other stock car drivers had trouble with a crown I was asked to do the repair.

So, in February 1990, I drove to Daytona where they were shooting some of the racing scenes. I was met by the medical director, who coordinated any work that a doctor had to perform, whether surgery, optometry or dentistry. He was a few years younger than me, very cordial, but strict about rules and regulations. When I arrived, one of the first things he said was that I would have to put my camera back in the car—it was a closed set and no photography was permitted.

I was escorted around the set, and was amazed at everything that went into making a motion picture. There must have been hundreds of people arranging props, setting up the lighting and moving equipment from one place to another. I watched some of the filming, which was brief compared to all the set-up time.

To my delight, I was introduced to Nicole Kidman, who told me she was scared of dentists, and Robert Duvall, one of my favorite actors of all time. He'd delivered standout performances in the *Godfather* movies and had a unforgettable role in the television miniseries *Lonesome Dove*.

When the lunch break was called, I saw people heading to a tent where hamburgers and hot dogs were being grilled. I was pretty hungry by this time, and moved to join the crowd.

"Where are you going?" the medical director asked me.

"To get something to eat."

"That's for regular people," he said. "We don't eat with them."

I thought I was a regular person. All I wanted was a hamburger.

My escort said, "We eat at the star's trailer," and led the way. He told me that our lunch would be prepared to order by Tom Cruise's personal French chef.

We fell into a much shorter line than at the burger tents. When we neared the window where orders were being placed, I said, "What should I ask for?"

"Anything you want."

"Oh, I think I'm in the mood for lobster linguini," I joked.

"No problem."

"I was just kidding!"

"They'll make it for you. Won't take long at all."

A voice directly behind me called out, "I'll have the same!" I turned around and there was Robert Duvall. When we got our meals, I sat down at a table with the medical director and Duvall headed to his trailer carrying his dish of lobster linguini. As he passed by, he nodded to me and said, "Good choice."

Shooting on the film wrapped up early and I left for home. To make up for me not being allowed to take photographs, I was given a copy of the day's shooting script.

I was later called upon to provide dental care when other movies were filming in Florida. One of them was *Monster*, the story of the female serial killer, for which Charlize Theron won an Academy Award. Several scenes were shot at a roller skating rink in Casselberry, a few miles from my office, and I provided treatment and consultations.

In the years that followed, I went on to be involved with a number of movie and television productions. That first experience with *Days of Thunder* will always be special, though, and it only came about because Greg Sacks wouldn't trust his teeth to any other dentist.

***

Although I was much more accomplished as a spectator than as an athlete, I participated in sports myself. I played some softball, bowled and resumed the long-distance running that I'd given up in high school.

While I was in the Navy, I began running several miles a day and competed in some 5k and 10k races. I continued this routine when I opened my dental practice. During lunch times, I would run through the neighborhood, then come back to the office, shower and change, and be ready for my afternoon patients. On weekends, I occasionally ran races. My times were never great—my ever-present camera hampered me a bit—but I enjoyed the exercise and the challenge.

In the summer of 1992, I had just completed a 10k in downtown Orlando when I saw a friend of mine, another local dentist, on a cot in the medical tent. His wife was standing nervously by and I asked her what had happened. "He collapsed during the race," she said. "But they say he should be fine."

"What was Tom doing a running a race?" I asked in disbelief. Tom weighed about three hundred pounds and never exercised.

"He's getting ready for the New York Marathon."

"*What?*"

His wife explained, "He has a patient—a marathon runner—with a serious condition and the man refused to get it corrected. Tom made him a deal: If he got the treatment, Tom would run the New York Marathon. Tom's a man of his word, so he's going to keep his part of the agreement."

"All right," I said. "Here's what we'll do: Tom is going to train with me for the next few months and we'll run it together." I had never run a marathon before, but I figured it's basically the same as a 10k except about four times as long.

Tom quickly recovered from the Orlando race and the two of us began training. I relied on the methods I'd been taught by my high school track coach. We both built up our muscles and endurance, Tom lost a little weight, and at the end of October we flew to New York confident that we could survive the ordeal.

On November first, we hit the ground running in Staten Island and 26.2 miles later we both crossed the finish line in Central Park. My time was five hours, two minutes, and thirty-five seconds. I could have easily done it in under five hours, but I carried a little 35 mm camera in my fanny pack and often stopped along the way to take photos. Tom suffered no ill effects from the race and his patient went ahead with the treatment that he needed.

Tom and I enjoyed the experience so much that we competed there again two years later, and again we both made it to the finish line. I decided to try some other courses, and went on to run the Disney, Marine Corps, Las Vegas and London marathons.

My entry in the London marathon came about through the American Diabetes Association. I had raised a significant amount of money for the charity and as a reward was given a trip to London to run the marathon in 1999.

April in London is rainy, though. The day before the race, I slipped on a wet patch of pavement during a practice run and broke a bone in my foot. I intended to carry on anyway, and successfully eluded the medical staff who were evaluating competitors for injuries or health conditions.

Thanks to large quantities of determination and Motrin, I managed to hobble my way through the course. It wasn't the soundest medical decision I'd ever made, but there was no long-term damage to my foot and I crossed the finish line in front of Buckingham Palace.

Less than a year later, with my foot fully mended, I completed my second Disney marathon in Orlando. Initially I ran alone, until I spotted a heavily tattooed guy keeping pace not far from me. I drew closer to check out his skin art and saw that his tattoos all incorporated a New York Yankees logo.

"Nice ink," I commented. "I'm a Yankee fan, too."

He told me that he sold hot dogs and peanuts at Yankee Stadium and had a tattoo for every World Series the team had won, a total of twenty-five at that time. Having found a kindred spirit, we talked baseball the rest of the route.

When I finished, I discovered that the hot dog vendor wasn't the only one at Epcot who had worked at Yankee Stadium. Standing off to the side, his eyes directed at the incoming runners, was Don Mattingly. He was sporting a beard, and his cap was pulled low, but I recognized him as "Donnie Baseball." Mattingly had had a spectacular fourteen-year career as the Yankees' first baseman and was a fan favorite.

Huffing from the race, I walked over to him. "Excuse me," I said. "I don't mean to intrude, but aren't you Don Mattingly?"

He seemed surprised to be recognized, but acknowledged that he was.

"Did you run the race?" I asked.

"No, my wife is." He kept an eye on the runners still trickling in. "To tell you the truth, I'm getting a little worried. I expected her a while ago."

"I can find her for you," I offered.

"How?"

I introduced myself, told him I was a local dentist who ran races regularly in Orlando, and that I knew the officials who could track his wife's location on the route. "Follow me," I said.

Mattingly hesitated a moment, then shrugged and followed me to one of the administration tents. The friendly greetings I received from race officials who knew me reassured him that I wasn't a crackpot. He was also reassured that his wife was okay when they confirmed for him that she was still running the course.

Mattingly thanked me for my help and I left him alone to await his wife. Before I did, though, I asked if I could have a photo taken with him and he agreed. Once again, the camera that I always ran with came in handy.

A few months later, I saw Mattingly at the Yankees spring training camp. He had been retired as a player for five years and was now a hitting instructor for the team during spring training. The beard was gone—George Steinbrenner had a rule against beards—and he was about to board the team bus outside the park.

By now, I'd had the photo we'd taken at Epcot enlarged. I called out to him, "Don!"

He was on the first step of the bus, but when he heard my voice he stepped back down and came over to where I was standing. "Dr. B. from Disney," he greeted me. "Nice to see you again." We spoke briefly and he autographed the photo.

I completed my last marathon in Las Vegas in 2006. Some people think that jogging twenty-six miles must make for a boring five hours. But I somehow managed to run into some interesting situations during my races.

***

When the Yankees moved their spring training site from Ft. Lauderdale to Tampa in the spring of 1996, they quickly became an integral part of the Tampa Bay community. The area wouldn't have its own major-league team for two more years, so Legends Field was the place to go for baseball.

Yankees' owner George Steinbrenner was a long-time resident of Tampa and contributed to a number of local charities. He was an especially strong supporter of the Boys & Girls Clubs of Tampa Bay. To benefit these clubs, he established the New York Yankees luncheon, which took place in March.

The annual event was held in a ritzy waterfront hotel. Admission cost a few hundred dollars, and guests could pay extra for a half-hour autograph session before the meal. After lunch, there were presentations and an auction. Every current Yankee player was required to attend and there were always some old-timers as well. This was an event I looked forward to every spring. It was a chance to meet the players, gather with other Yankee fans and support a great cause.

At the 1998 luncheon, I brought along a photo that I had taken of Derek Jeter. He was three seasons into what would be a twenty-year Hall of Fame career. He spent all of it with the Yankees, served as team captain for more than a decade and established himself as one of the team's all-time greats. I eagerly sought him in the autograph room, but he wasn't there. Jeter had missed the session.

He arrived in time for the luncheon, however, since Steinbrenner was a stickler about that. During the meal, I saw Jeter get up and head out of the banquet room. I quickly went into the hallway, photo in hand, hoping I could catch him. I spotted him walking with another ballplayer, and I called to him, "How's Casey Close?"

Jeter pulled up short and came over to me. "You're a friend of Casey?" Close was a former minor leaguer and Derek Jeter's agent.

"No," I admitted. "I can't lie to you. I only know he's a good friend of yours and I thought that would get your attention. I was hoping to see you at the autograph session." I pulled out the photo and introduced myself. "I think this is a great shot of you," I went on, "and I'd love to hang it up in my office if you'd be kind enough to sign it."

Jeter appeared stunned. "Well, honesty is certainly a new approach." He reached for the picture and studied it for a moment. "Nice," he said approvingly, and with a flourish autographed it "To Dr. B." I sent him a copy of the print a day later. Over the years, he remembered me and signed quite a few items.

On July 18, 1999, I was in Yankee Stadium for Yogi Berra Day. The Yankees would be playing the Montreal Expos and Joe Sardano had gotten us box seats behind the Yankees dugout through his connections at General Electric. After Don Larson, who had pitched the only perfect World Series game, threw out the ceremonial first pitch to Berra, Yankees' pitcher David Cone went out and pitched a perfect game of his own against the Expos. Toward the end of the game, Derek Jeter took off his batting glove and tossed it toward where I was sitting. I caught it and realized this was quite a memento from a historic game. Leaning forward, I said to a little boy a couple rows in front of me, "I think this is for you," and handed him the glove. Jeter caught my eye and gave me a thumbs up.

After Tampa was awarded an American League franchise, I often went to Tropicana Field to see the Yankees play the Devil Rays. By then, Jeter and I had seen each other several times, and he would take a minute to exchange a few words with me or sign a photo. On one occasion, I was with John Sittig, the Coopers & Lybrand accountant who had arranged for my family and me to visit Legends Field when it first opened. John had his two young sons with him and they both sported Yankees batting helmets.

"You think you could get Derek Jeter to sign the helmets?" John asked me. "You seem to have an in with him."

"I can try." I worked my way down the aisle with John's two boys in front of me. I caught Jeter's attention and pointed at the tops of the boys helmets. He waved us down to the railing, where he talked briefly with the boys and autographed their helmets. The boys were thrilled, John was grateful, and I was happy that, thanks to Derek Jeter, I could return the kindness that John had shown me years earlier.

***

Some of the greatest Yankees stars were former members of the Boston Red Sox, from Babe Ruth and Waite Hoyt to Sparky Lyle and Wade Boggs. Hard-throwing Roger Clemens, who'd won three Cy Young awards with Boston and two more with Toronto, became the latest in this line when he signed with New York in 1999.

A few weeks after Clemens' move to the Yankees, I received a phone call from my friend Steve Priest, a professional sports photographer based in Orlando. He was the official photographer of the major-league umpires and had great connections. "Don't tell anyone," he said, "but Roger Clemens is throwing out the first pitch at Tinker Field tonight. I'll get you credentials and you bring anything you want him to sign."

The scheduled game was a high school contest involving Lake Highland Prep, which was coached by Frank Viola, another Cy Young award winner. He and Clemens had pitched together on the Red Sox and remained close friends.

As a special surprise for Viola's players, Clemens had agreed to throw out the game's first pitch.

I showed up early, Steve gave me press credentials and I was able to go onto the field. Clemens and Viola were both in cheerful moods, and Clemens signed the items I'd brought with me. He also went to the railing and gave autographs to delighted fans who hadn't expected to see major league baseball's best pitcher at a high school game.

I spoke with both pitchers for a little while. Clemens and Viola talked about Braves pitcher John Smoltz with admiration, and they updated each other on their golf games. After I'd taken all the photos that I wanted, I thanked them and said to Clemens, "I'll see you at the Yankee luncheon next week." It was time for the Yankees annual spring training event.

"No you won't," he replied. "I'm pitching against the Phillies that afternoon. I'm not going to any luncheon."

"But Steinbrenner makes all the players go," I said.

"Not me," Clemens insisted.

A week later, I drove to Tampa and went to the pre-lunch autograph session. There was Roger Clemens, not looking happy but signing autographs at his table.

When he saw me approach, he sighed, "Don't say a word, Dr. B." Then he signed the photos I'd taken at Tinker Field. Clemens had discovered that George Steinbrenner's edicts were not negotiable.

***

Two years later, in March of 2001, I was again at the Yankees luncheon, but this time I wanted George Steinbrenner's autograph. I had a copy of the *Sports Illustrated* issue that featured a cover photo of Steinbrenner dressed as Napoleon astride a white horse. Although he was called "The Boss," he certainly acted more as an emperor and I thought the picture captured him perfectly.

I tried to approach his table but was blocked by security. Seated next to Steinbrenner was Supreme Court Justice Anton Scalia and there were police and guards all over the place. "Nobody's allowed past this point," I was told.

Undeterred, I called to Steinbrenner, "Don Dizney says hello!" Donald Dizney was founder and president of a major medical corporation, breeder of thoroughbred racehorses, and had owned a couple of professional football teams. He also happened to be a long-time friend of George Steinbrenner.

Steinbrenner summoned a plainclothes officer, spoke a few words to him, and I was ushered inside the security cordon. "How's Don doing?" the Boss asked me.

"Hanging in there," I said, with no idea whether or not that was true, for I had never met the man. "If you don't mind, Mr. Steinbrenner, would you sign this for me?'

"Any friend of Don Dizney is a friend of mine," he said, as he signed the magazine cover.

I thanked him and retreated to my assigned table. I was happy at my success, and enjoyed the rest of the luncheon in the elegant banquet hall of the Marriott Waterside Hotel. It seemed there couldn't be any better place to be, with outstanding food, attentive staff and among the company of the New York Yankees.

I didn't know that in only one month I would begin a journey that would lead me to drastically different surroundings and a very peculiar kind of team.

10. Survivor Africa

Once again, it all started by me opening my big mouth.

My office manager Dawn used to come in on Thursday mornings and talk about the latest episode of a CBS reality show called *Survivor*. She was a huge fan of the program and liked to tell the staff about the latest conflicts among the contestants and who was voted off. I didn't watch much television, had never seen the show and was too preoccupied with treating my patients to be interested in her recaps.

Dawn was convinced that I would like the show if I understood the premise and she tried to explain it to me. I didn't pay close attention, but apparently it involved some naked guy and a bunch of other people doing silly challenges on an island. Whomever survived the longest would win a million dollars. I said something dismissive, probably to the effect that it sounded like *Gilligan's Island* with party games.

"You think *you* could do it?" Dawn seemed a bit miffed that I'd ridiculed her favorite show.

"In a New York minute," I said emphatically.

Then I went to see to my next patient and thought no more about Dawn's TV viewing habits. The next time I came to the front desk, she handed me a sheaf of papers. "Here, let's see how you do," she said with a smile. She had downloaded and printed an application to be a contestant on *Survivor*. "You'll send this in, right?"

Now I was stuck. I always believed that if you boast you can do something, you had to back it up. "I will," I promised. On the bright side, I figured all I was doing was sending in an application and the odds of actually getting picked were astronomically small.

I put the application in my brief case and forgot about it. A few days before it was due, in mid-April 2001, Dawn helpfully reminded me and printed out another copy. She was not going to let me off the hook. But nor was I going to back down.

The written application was about a dozen pages long and I filled it out completely. Then I saw that I also had to submit a three-minute video, and I had no idea what to do about that. I'm no videographer, I didn't know what to tape for three minutes, and it turned out that the old VHS recorder that I had used when my children were young no longer worked. I called around, but wasn't able to get hold of a working video camera until the last day.

I brought the camera into my office and announced to Dawn and the rest of my staff that I would be taping the video after the last patient's appointment if they wanted to stay and watch. They all did, especially Dawn—I think she wanted to witness me making a fool of myself.

At the end of the workday, the video shoot began. The production was a rush job because the application had to be postmarked that same day. I had no script, didn't know what the video was supposed to include and the minutes were ticking by. One of my staff said, "Just be yourself."

Well, that made it easy for me. I stood at my office door and Dawn began filming.

"I'm Dr. Carl Bilancione," I began. "Why should I be on Survivor? Because I *am* a survivor. Dentists have the highest suicide rate of any profession, but since I'm talking to you obviously I haven't killed myself. We have one of the highest divorce rates, but I've been happily married for twenty-six years." I walked across my office to point out a big picture of me crossing the finish line of the 1992 New York Marathon. "When I start something, I finish." I lifted the front of my scrub shirt and showed my roll of excess belly. "I can run with this and still complete any race." I had the camera pan around my office and concluded, "This is my office and this is who I am. I have no idea if this has been three minutes, but I'm telling you: If you want high ratings, pick me. If you don't, *fuggedaboudit*."

I packed up the videotape and the application and brought it to the post office for overnight delivery. When I got home, I mentioned to Deborah that I'd applied for *Survivor*. "You did what?" she asked, with a what-did-you-do-now sigh.

I told her about the application and the video.

"They're going to pick you," she said. "So be sure you want to do it."

"No way. I'm a forty-six-year-old overweight dentist—I don't think that's what they're looking for on a show like this. Besides, they must have a million people applying. I just had to show Dawn that I was willing. Now it's done."

About two weeks later, I got a letter that I almost threw out with the junk mail. The envelope had "SEG" on the return address, which meant nothing to me. But then I noticed it was from Santa Monica, California, where I had sent the application.

The "SEG" stood for Survivor Entertainment Group, and the letter informed me that I was one of eight hundred people selected to move on in the interview process. Seventy thousand people had initially applied altogether. There were sixteen locations around the country for this second stage, with fifty applicants scheduled at each site. Mine was to be Miami.

By now, I had learned more about the show and was getting excited about the prospect. I had been thinking of taking a photographic safari to Africa, and it turned out that the location for this season of *Survivor* would be Africa. Also, the contestants tended to starve while they're in the competition and I wanted to lose some of the two hundred thirty pounds I was lugging around. The idea of competing appealed to me, too; I simply love a challenge. So it was on to Miami!

***

Applicants for this round of interviews were given appointments for a specific day and time at their assigned location. We were responsible for our own travel arrangements and expenses. I flew down to Miami on a warm day in May and took a cab to the local CBS affiliate where the interviews were being held.

When I arrived, I cheerfully introduced myself to a scowling young man seated behind the registration desk. "You're early," he snapped. "You were told *not* to be early." He pointed to a waiting area where half a dozen people were already seated. "Sit there. Do *not* speak."

I complied, and wondered why the production company would make such an unpleasant person our initial contact.

The guy seemed to think he was welcoming new Marine recruits at Parris Island. I eventually caught on that there was a psychological game taking place; we were constantly observed to see how we responded to various situations. None of the production staff told us their names, and only a few revealed their job titles. It seemed they wanted to keep us confused and off guard.

Along with the rest of the group, I maintained silence for several hours. We'd been told that speaking to another applicant would be grounds for disqualification. Although I sat with the others, I did not fit in. They were all in their twenties and looked like models. If that was what the producers were looking for, I thought, I might as well head back to Orlando.

In fact, I *would* have to head back soon because it was long past my appointed time. I checked with the wannabe drill sergeant at the front desk, who would only tell me what I already knew: The interviews were running late. Fortunately, I had eaten before I got to the studio; there were no food or beverages available other than a water fountain.

At one point, I was permitted to go out to the parking lot for some air. A few other applicants were out doing the same, and we tried to keep some distance between us so that no one would think we were fraternizing. As I started to go back inside, a petite young woman with a clipboard opened the door and called to me, "I need to speak to you!"

Oh no, I thought. She probably thinks I was talking to somebody and now I am going to be disqualified before I even had an interview.

"We're running about three hours late," she said. "What time were you scheduled for?"

I gave her my name and told her I needed to get back to Orlando for work the next day.

"You're the dentist who did that video!" she cried. "We're all looking forward to speaking with you. The energy and the vibe you had were fantastic—I hope you can turn it on again when we're taping."

"What do you mean 'turn it on'?" I said. "I wouldn't know how to turn it *off*. I'm the same way twenty-four-seven. What you see is what you get."

A while later, she informed me that it was finally my turn. It was late, but early enough that I should still be able to catch my flight home. The proceedings took place on the set of a talk show. There was a cameraman to record everything and a sound technician who rigged me with a microphone. Another woman, obviously senior to the one who'd escorted me, conducted the interview. She did not introduce herself, but I assumed she was a casting director or some level of producer. While getting herself situated, she mentioned that my video had grabbed her attention because of what'd I'd said about dentists' suicide and divorce rates—she was currently dating a dental student and wondered if there was cause for concern.

When the tape started rolling, she began with, "Tell me why you want to do this."

I decided not to tell her that I'd simply been goaded into it by Dawn. "Three reasons," I answered. "It's in Africa, and I want to see Africa. Also, I want to lose weight. And it's a competition; I like to test myself in competitions to see what I'm capable of."

She looked at me in disbelief. "*Those* are your reasons?"

"Yes, why?"

"Not the million dollar prize?"

"No, I'm not really motivated by money. I just want to live a good life, meet new people and have fun."

"A *million dollars*," she repeated.

"More like six hundred thousand after taxes," I said. "Sure, money's nice, and for the younger contestants it could change their lives. But it wouldn't change mine. Win or lose, I'm going to be a dentist with a nice house and a loving family."

She asked me quite a few additional questions which I answered honestly. Then she called to someone who had been sitting and listening out of view. "Do you have any questions, Craig?" That was the first name that anyone had uttered all day.

A thin, dark-haired man about my age joined us. I later learned that he was Craig Piligian, co-executive producer of *Survivor* and a major figure in reality television programming. Among the shows Piligian went on to create were *Dirty Jobs, American Chopper* and *The Ultimate Fighter*.

Piligian was very friendly and we spoke for a while. When the interview was finished, I asked, "When will I hear if I made it to the next round?"

"In about a week," he said.

I shook my head. "That doesn't work for me."

"Excuse me?"

"I'm a one-man dental practice. Patients come in from all over the country to see me and I can't reschedule them on short notice. I'd really need to know ASAP if I'm going to California."

"Are you serious?"

"Yes. I'd love to do the show, but I need to be sure my patients are taken care of first."

Piligian said a cordial good-bye, and I left the interview room pretty sure that a trip to Africa was not in my immediate future.

The assistant who escorted me to the exit whispered, "I can't believe you said that to him. Nobody's ever done that before."

I caught the flight back to Orlando that evening. Shortly after I got into the house, Craig Piligian called to tell me I was going to California.

***

It turned out that I wasn't the only one scheduled to be going someplace. During my application process for *Survivor*, my father called me. "Look Carl," he said. "I'm gonna be going away for a while and I want you to hear it from me."

"Where to?"

"Trenton—the penitentiary." He sounded as matter-of-fact as if he was simply going to Uncle Sal's hunting cabin for the weekend. "There was a crime at the docks and it was on my watch. The feds wanted me to name names, I refused, so they're making an example of me. Three months, no big deal."

I didn't ask any questions. I'd known since childhood that my father did not like to be questioned. And it would have been fruitless to do so anyway. My father was pretty much the poster boy for omerta.

The only details I learned were through published media reports. In 1995, two million dollars worth of perfume were stolen from Global Terminal on the Bayonne docks, where my father worked as the union field boss. The Waterfront Commission of New York Harbor received dozens of tips identifying Carlo Bilancione and others as being involved in the theft. The FBI and U.S. Customs began a multi-year probe, and in September of 2000 my father and one of his colleagues pleaded guilty to conspiracy to steal an interstate shipment of goods. Now the time had come for him to serve his sentence.

It was a bit odd. My father was able to tell me that he was going to prison, but I could say nothing to him about where I would be heading. *Survivor* candidates were prohibited from revealing that they were being considered for the show.

***

I thought I was applying for a television show, not to be a secret agent. The strict protocols established for the *Survivor* selection process in California would have done any of the intelligence agencies proud.

All of the travel and living arrangements were made by the show's producers. I was allowed to tell Deborah that I would be in Santa Monica for two weeks, but could not reveal the name of my hotel. Nor could I tell my staff where I would be, but my dental office would remain open and a colleague would cover for me.

When I arrived in Los Angeles, a shuttle brought me from the airport to the hotel. I was met by a stern young man who had been charged with orienting me to the process. He first informed me that I was no longer "Carl Bilancione" and assigned me an alias. I would be living in a secret location with a secret identity, which made me feel as if I'd entered the Witness Protection Program.

He gave me some of the most important rules: No talking with other applicants, no cell phones, no visitors. There were fifty finalists, all of whom had to remain sequestered in the hotel and were prohibited from having any interaction with each other.

After handing me my room key, the young man said, "You will find a package on your bed. Familiarize yourself with the contents and follow the instructions to a T."

I joked, "Is this like *Mission Impossible*, where it self-destructs after I've read it?"

"Not funny!" he snapped. How dare I make fun of something that he clearly believed to as sensitive as the nuclear football.

The room was quite comfortable, a one-bedroom suite with a living area and a refrigerator. The package on the bed was large; it included several binders with instructions, information and an endless number of schedules. Almost every minute would be governed by schedules: mealtimes, psychological tests, physical examinations, interviews, access to the hotel's workout room and breaks. There were also repeated reminders not to speak to other applicants, but to expect members from the production team to approach us at any time. There was a small army of producers, casting directors, assistants and interns marching about the hotel.

I discovered the next morning that the favorite time for spontaneous questioning was during meals. Since we weren't permitted to fraternize, no one in the final fifty could sit at the same table as another applicant. I had brought a little notebook with me, and as I looked around the restaurant I jotted down some observations.

An associate producer soon came and sat down across from me. "What are you doing?" she asked. The production staff was more forthcoming with their names and titles than they had been in Miami.

"Writing down my guesses for who you're going to pick." I didn't know their names so I used brief descriptions like "guy with crewcut" or "blonde with snake tattoo."

She asked me to point them out and explain my reasoning, which I did. "Interesting," was her only comment.

During most meals, a producer would come by and do some probing before moving on to another table. I imagine they reported the conversations to a higher-up.

Much of the time during the first week was spent with formal testing. Just as when I was in school, I took a seat up front and was always the first to finish. What made it easy for me was that I answered questions honestly and didn't waste any time trying to figure out which answers the producers would most like to hear.

One exam nearly eliminated me from contention, however, and that was my physical. My blood pressure was higher than the examining physician thought safe. He considered failing me, but after consulting my cardiologist in Florida gave me a clean bill of health.

Midway through our stay, we were given permission to walk around in Santa Monica during a designated period of time. We had to avoid any contact with other contestants, and were warned that we would be followed and watched. It was comical to see fifty people walking around and continually crossing to the other side of the street or ducking into stores so that no one would think we were breaking the rule!

Near the end of the two weeks, we had a couple of quiet days. I assumed that all of our tests and evaluations were being reviewed and some decisions were being made about who was still in contention.

Ellen, one of the nicest of the production staff, knocked on my door. "You have another interview," she said brightly. "We're taking you to the CBS studio." That had to be a good sign, I thought. If I had been eliminated, there was no reason for another interview.

The set up for the interview was intended to be intimidating. About twelve executives, all with clipboards, sat in tall director's chairs in a semicircle facing me. I had been given a low seat, so I felt like a kindergartner looking up at my teachers. One of my interviewers was Craig Piligian, who greeted me warmly and said he had enjoyed meeting me in Miami. Another was the show's other executive producer, Mark Burnett, also very friendly whom I was meeting for the first time. And the top boss was there: Les Moonves, President of CBS Entertainment.

The interview progressed smoothly and I answered their questions honestly. Like a jury, the twelve people facing me made notes.

Then Burnett said bluntly, "You know, you're kind of chubby. Are you sure you're physically capable of doing this?"

One of the other producers answered for me. "He ran the London marathon with a broken foot," she told him. "And he finished."

"How did you do that?" Burnett asked.

"Because I don't know what it is to quit. It's all between the ears, Mark: If my mind says I can do it, my body will follow."

Les Moonves spoke up for the first time. "Before we go any further," he said. "I need to know if you're in the Mafia."

I was sure that question would be coming at some point. "If I was, you could do a new show called *Mafia Dentist*," I quipped.

There were a few nervous laughs, but not many.

"No," I said. "I'm not in the Mafia."

Mark Burnett jumped in. "We know about your father."

"Of course you do. I told you about him."

"You did?"

"There was a question on one of the forms asking if any unfavorable news might come out about me or my family while the show was on. I told you all about my father." One of the producers murmured to Burnett that what I'd said was true. "My father's life is not mine," I continued. "I know you must have done background checks on me, and I don't even have a speeding ticket on my record. I'm a *dentist*—hell, I'm the head of Peer Review and Ethics for the Greater Orlando Dental Society."

"You're not embarrassed?" asked another one of the twelve.

I was getting annoyed. "*I've* never done anything to be embarrassed about. I worked my way through college and dental school, served in the Navy, and built a successful dental practice to provide a good life for me and my family. What the hell do I have to be embarrassed about?"

The people in the director's chairs exchanged some uncomfortable looks. But they had to raise the issue, I suppose, and they got my answer.

After a few more routine questions, Burnett asked, "If you went on the show, what would you want your luxury item to be?" Contestants were permitted one personal item that they could bring from home.

"A camera," I immediately replied.

Another producer said, just as quickly, "Absolutely not. Cameras are not allowed."

"I don't want to take pictures of the show, just Africa. That's one of the main reasons I want to go."

She shook her head in an adamant "no."

Addressing Burnett, I said, "I'll make you an offer you can't refuse."

With a hint of a smile, he asked, "What's the offer?"

"I will label all the film and give it to you to hold. You don't give it back to me until the last episode of the show has aired."

"No way," the other producer insisted. "We could never allow that."

The interview soon wrapped up, and everyone thanked me for coming and for applying to the show. Then I was driven back to the hotel, where we were only scheduled to stay a couple more days.

Around six o'clock, there was a knock at my door. It was Ellen again and she was beaming. "Congratulations! You're one of the twenty! I'm going to take you to get your inoculations."

"Twenty?" I was happy at being selected, but a little confused. "I thought only sixteen make the show."

"That's true. But we have four alternates in case one of the sixteen drops out."

"Am I an alternate or a contestant?"

"I can't tell you that. They haven't even told me. I only know who the twenty are."

"So I might go through all this and not even go to Africa?"

"That's correct."

"Then I'm not doing it. Either I'm on the show or I'm not. None of this limbo stuff."

Ellen appeared dumbfounded. "Nobody's ever turned us down before. I'll have to call Mark."

She left, and less than half an hour later Mark Burnett called me. "You're one of the sixteen, so go get your shots. And you can bring a camera."

***

With only two weeks until I would be leaving the country, I returned to Florida to make my preparations—and there was a *lot* to do. I had been given a long checklist of items to bring, an even longer list of prohibited items, a contract that I needed to sign and a rulebook.

I was allowed to tell Deborah and our children where I was going, and that I would be incommunicado for about seven weeks. All contestants had to remain in Africa for the duration of filming, since coming back early would reveal who had been eliminated. Deborah was supportive, as always, but concerned that I might injure my hand and not be able to continue practicing dentistry. Bryan thought it sounded like a great adventure, and Jessica worried that I might be eaten by a lion.

I hired another dentist to fill in for me while I was gone, and called Mark Burnett to tell him that I would have to inform my staff where I was. He agreed, and they all signed nondisclosure agreements with the production company. I didn't even tell my parents where I was going.

Among the items I had to bring were duplicate sets of everything I would wear. The second set of clothing was for a body double. When stations begin broadcasting teasers for the upcoming season, the episodes haven't been filmed yet. Body doubles are used, and they're filmed from behind as they walk through the woods or climb a tree.

I flew back to California on the Fourth of July. I had everything on the *Survivor* checklist as well as two cameras and thirty-six rolls of film. All of the contestants spent one night at a hotel near the airport and we departed the next day for Amsterdam. Now that I saw who else had been selected, I noticed that most of the predictions I had made in the Santa Monica hotel were correct.

When we landed in Amsterdam, the men and women were sent to different rooms at the Amsterdam Sheraton to await the flight to Africa. Our seats were assigned by the producers, and for the most part we were still separated from each other. Somehow, they assigned me a seat next to another contestant, Jessie Camacho. We were practically neighbors; she was a graduate of Winter Park High School and had been named Orlando's "Miss Puerto Rico." We only got to chat briefly before someone caught the mistake and I was moved to another row.

Left alone on the rest of the flight to Nairobi, I imagined what might be facing me. I was excited to see the wildlife of Africa and energized by the idea of the competition. But I also knew that we were heading into a tough terrain where survival really could be a challenge.

At the same time that I was on that flight, my father was confined to a prison cell in Trenton, New Jersey. The thought occurred to me that for the next month or two he might actually have the more comfortable accommodations.

11. What the Hell Did I Get Myself Into?

I had dreamed of seeing Africa for years, and eagerly looked forward to photographing lions, elephants, zebras and antelope. I hoped that I might even be lucky enough to see a rhino or a hippo. While I anticipated all sorts of fascinating and exotic sights in Africa, one thing I had never imagined encountering was machine guns.

Our eight-hour flight from Amsterdam to Kenya, on the east coast of Africa, was nearly over. The plane dropped altitude, and through the clouds I glimpsed lush jungle, open savanna and roiling rivers. As we approached Nairobi, high-rise apartments, office buildings and hotels dominated the landscape; the Kenyan capital was a modern city with a population double that of Orlando. It was also a city of extreme poverty, with extensive slums and mountains of garbage crowding the edge of the airport. Those nice hotels we had seen from the sky were surrounded by barbed wire fences and patrolled by armed guards.

At seven in the morning on July sixth, we touched down at Jomo Kenyatta International Airport. When the passengers disembarked the plane, most went to the terminal as usual. But each *Survivor* contestant was pulled aside by the show's production staff. We were rounded up and taken into a government facility, where we were ushered into a secure holding area.

We spent four hours sitting in mandated silence, with armed soldiers milling around us. Each soldier wore a

174

camouflage uniform with a black beret, and each was equipped with a terrifying submachine gun. Some had them hanging on slings from their shoulder straps; others held them at the ready. Looking at all those lethal weapons, I thought that no lion or leopard could be any scarier.

I don't know why we were being held in a government building, but I do know that production of the show was coordinated with the Kenyan authorities. More than half of the Shaba National Reserve, one of the country's most popular tourist destinations, was being sealed off for four months to accommodate the filming of *Survivor*. I can't imagine that kind of access came cheaply. I assume that we were kept away from the main airport because the producers wanted to isolate us from the public and the paparazzi. The show's first two seasons had been wildly popular, and there was worldwide media interest in the upcoming one. *Survivor's* producers were determined to limit access and maintain secrecy.

Shortly before noon we were escorted to a runway and divided into two groups. These weren't our assigned teams yet. There were simply so many production staff and film crew traveling with the contestants that we needed to take two planes.

We boarded and took off for a fifty-minute flight to the reserve where the competition would take place. I was happy to leave the soldiers behind and eager to see the Africa that I had imagined for so long.

***

Shaba National Reserve, in the center of Kenya, is a magnificent nature preserve with forests, mountains, grasslands and a winding river, all dominated by a dark, jagged volcano that rises more than a mile high. It had been used for filming the movies *Born Free* and *Out of Africa,* and would now be the location for *Survivor Africa.*

Our planes came down onto a dirt landing strip where we were greeted by an enthusiastic group of beautifully adorned Masai. They wore traditional red garments along with colorful beads and jewelry. Unfortunately, there was little time to interact with them. We were quickly put into jeeps and bounced across miles of rocky ground that pretended to be a road.

We arrived at a mountainside base camp that would be our home until the start of the actual competition. Each of us had a little pup tent for sleeping, with a canvas overhang out front. Under the shade of the canopy were a small wooden table and a canvas-back folding chair that would serve as an outdoor living room. Our assigned quarters had already been set up and our belongings distributed. Bottled water had also been provided—essential in the hot African sun. My tent was #5 and there was a sign on my table that read "C. Bil." Next to my tent was the trail that led to the camp toilet, which was nothing more than a hole in the ground.

A rustic stone lodge overlooking the valley had also been constructed at the site, and production staff escorted us there for lunch. Producers Mark Burnett and Craig Piligian welcomed us and gave us an overview of our schedule. For the next three days we would be undergoing a crash course in survival training with a couple of professional instructors. We were allowed to speak to the instructors, but still prohibited from any conversation with another contestant. Each of us was issued a manual with the catchy title *Survival Handbook for Survivor Africa, Kenya, East Africa, 2001* which we were to study thoroughly. The remainder of that afternoon was spent in reviewing a myriad of rules and conducting individual interviews.

During my meeting with the producers, Burnett brought up a subject that I thought had been settled during my California interview. "We've done some more checking into your father," he said. "We were really blown away by what we learned." He hesitated. "But *you're* not in the Mafia, right?"

"If I was, *you'd* be working for *me*," I joked.

Burnett and Piligian both laughed and neither of them raised the matter again. Then they asked about my approach to the game. I told them that I would not lie about anything even if it was in my strategic interest to do so. I had patients who trusted my word; I didn't want them to see me being deceitful in the show and then wondering if I was honest in my practice. The producers said that I could go further in the game if I was more flexible on that point, but I told them that deceit wasn't an option for me. Win or lose, I would play with integrity.

They then suggested that I at least keep my profession a secret from the other players. Burnett said that if I revealed that I was a dentist, the others would assume I was wealthy and didn't deserve to win the prize money. My thinking was that if my teammates knew I had medical experience, they would believe I had some valuable skills and would want to keep me around longer. It turned out that the producers had a better read on the contestants than I did.

When the interviews were over, our first evening in base camp was free. Some of us read the manuals we'd been given, while others sat on the camp chairs outside our pup tents silently sizing each other up. Finally, I crawled into my little tent to sleep my first night in Africa. Although the nocturnal wildlife was raucous, and the tent stifling, utter exhaustion enabled me to sleep well.

We spent the next three days learning essential skills from a couple of experienced survivalists. One lesson was on how to start a fire without a match; we would need fire to boil drinking water and to discourage predators. We also learned about the poisonous snakes we might encounter, how to identify the droppings of various animals and how to read the prints of various species.

As much as I tried to absorb all the information, I didn't feel that three days was really enough training to ensure survival on the savanna. But I was pretty confident that I could now identify whatever kind of animal was about to devour me.

***

The day after our survival training concluded, we were woken early in the morning with the announcement "The game is on!" We were instructed to drink as much water as we could hold and gather our belongings. Then the contestants were put onto a transport truck that was probably used more for soldiers than civilians. It was a drab, uncomfortable vehicle with a canvas roof and open sides. Our seats were assigned and we were not permitted to speak.

Jeff Probst, the host of the show, was with us and he narrated the introduction to the new season for the show's opening montage. We drove through the bush for hours while he described the hardships we would be facing. There was a lot of repetition since the film crew had to shoot numerous takes at a variety of distances and angles. Although Probst enumerated many perils—wild animals, lack of water, lack of food, heat exhaustion—there was a more urgent matter currently facing us. Before we got in the truck, we had guzzled all the water we possibly could and some of us now had bladders on the verge of bursting. Probst was annoyed by the interruption, but agreed to stop the truck for a bathroom break—not that there was an actual bathroom in the vicinity.

After resuming the journey, the truck continued for miles until it stopped again. The burly military man driving the truck yelled, "Get out! Get out!" We scrambled out of the truck and were directed toward two areas that had been set up, one for each of the tribes into which we would be divided.

We had to look for our names to see which tribe would be ours. Half were Boran and the other half Samburu, in honor of two real Kenyan tribes. I had been assigned to Samburu and joined the seven others in my group. At forty-six, I was the oldest of our tribe. I quickly bonded with Frank Garrison, a forty-three-year-old man from western New York. Unfortunately, Samburu developed two factions based on age. Four of us were in our forties, and the other four in their twenties. The age gap soon became a chasm.

Each tribe had its own shelter called a "boma." This was a rickety enclosure made of loosely piled acacia branches that had thorns about three inches long. Each boma was already about ninety percent completed when we arrived and we had to finish the construction before nightfall. The final structure was about six feet high, with no roof, and would do nothing to keep out rain, heat, cold or insects.

The main purpose of the boma was to ward off animals, since the acacia thorns would tear up their hides if they tried to break through. It might deter a squirrel, I thought, but it didn't look like it would provide much protection from a truly determined lion. What we needed was a blazing fire to keep the wildlife away. Relying on our newly learned survival skills, we made endless attempts at starting a fire—and failed completely.

That first night was so miserable that I couldn't sleep. The heat had been stifling during the day and now the temperature had plummeted to a numbing cold. As I sat shivering, I tried to appreciate the magnificence of the setting. With no city lights nearby, the darkness was complete and a million stars sparkled in the sky; it was intoxicating to stare up at them. And, for a while, there was a quiet and a calm that I had rarely experienced. But then the animals became active and the silence was shattered.

Lions roared not far away, and to me the boma looked like a fragile pile of sticks. Frank was awake, too, and I told him that I would keep lookout and let the tribe know of any imminent dangers. We failed to make fire again the second night, and I stayed up again on watch. I was not going to trust anybody with my life but myself. Sitting in the dark, listening to the roars and shrieks and growls of the wildlife that surrounded us, I repeatedly wondered: *What the hell did I get myself into?*

I don't believe I got a minute's sleep during the first forty-eight hours of the competition, and I knew that I wouldn't be able to last that way. Each tribe had been given a little medical kit; I examined its contents and found a monocular, which is like a small telescope. I took the device apart and removed the lens, which I realized could be used like a magnifying glass for starting a fire. Before I could give it a try, I was called for one of the individual interviews that were intercut with the group scenes. I handed the lens to my teammate Silas and he had a fire going by the time I got back.

Water was another serious challenge for us. The watering hole that provided our only drinking water was a vile cesspool of animal waste. To remove the big chunks, we first strained it through a running shirt that I had brought. Then we boiled what remained and drank the fetid liquid.

I still didn't get much sleep. The younger members of our tribe seemed to think that the fire would keep going like central heating and that the water would come from a magical fountain. Along with the other senior members, I was constantly gathering firewood, staying up to feed the fire during the night, and scooping and boiling water. The twenty-somethings thought we were showing off by working so hard, and in turn we thought they had little work ethic at all.

With fire and water resolved, the issue of food remained. There was simply too little of it. Our season of *Survivor* was later criticized for providing the players with so few calories that we had no energy and appeared lethargic—who wants to watch a bunch of sleepwalkers stumbling about? Filming would last thirty-nine days and we had barely enough food available to last ten. The supply consisted of a small stack of unlabeled cans. We didn't know what our dinner would be until we opened a random can. Then we'd pass it around, and each member of the team might have a mouthful of cherries or green beans. That would be it for the meal.

Every three days, the tribes had to face a challenge. Whichever team lost that contest would have to go to "tribal council" and vote off one of its members. Samburu won the first two, so we remained eight-strong going into Day Nine. Our team was intact, but not united; the rift between old and young had continued to grow. When we lost the third competition, both factions maneuvered to vote out a member of the other group and take control of the tribe.

On television, it appears that players walk directly from the boma to the tribal council location, but it's actually much more arduous. The process took about eight hours for us. We were marched around endlessly in the hot sun while being filmed from a helicopter. Then we had to wait until sundown for the lighting to be exactly right for the cameraman. Hot, exhausted and hungry generally leads to poor decision-making, but maybe the show's executives felt it made for better television.

As expected, the Samburu vote split four-to-four, with the younger members voting to expel me and the older ones voting to expel Lindsey. With the tie, Lindsey and I were each given a chance to plead our case to the rest of the team and try to change the voters' minds. It was useless; everyone's positions were so entrenched that not one vote was swayed. This had never happened before on *Survivor*. Filming came to a standstill while Mark Burnett tried to figure out a procedure for breaking the deadlock.

Finally, he decided to settle the matter by giving us a quiz based largely on the Survivor Manual. Lindsey and I went a number of rounds, only a few of which were broadcast, with each of us getting every answer wrong. Although I had read every page of the manual, my mind was simply shut down and I couldn't remember a thing. Then we came to a question on how to remove a tick, and my medical background caused me to give the wrong response. Lindsey had gotten a tick during the show which had been removed by pouring hot water on it, so she said that was the correct procedure. I couldn't imagine pouring hot water on a patient and said that it wasn't. Lindsey was credited with the win, and I was out.

***

Immediately after tribal council, I was filmed for my parting words, which was my final on-camera appearance of the program. That left me with about a month still to spend in Africa—and it provided me with the most enjoyable experiences of the entire trip.

In a production as extensive as *Survivor*, there are buildings and tents behind the film set that are never shown.

There had to be housing and meal services for the crew, areas to store and repair equipment, meeting rooms for conferences and medical facilities. After recording my final words of the show, I was led to one of the hidden tents. Two psychologists—the same ones who had spoken with us in California—were waiting to interview me.

One of them asked in that soothing, concerned tone unique to therapists and psychologists, "How do you feel, Carl? Are you depressed? Are you upset?"

"No, I'm not depressed," I said. "I'm disappointed because I let my tribe down. I could have helped them be successful in the coming challenges, and now I won't have a chance to do that."

The other psychologist asked, "What happened with the elimination test? I'm surprised someone as intelligent as you had trouble answering those questions."

"My brain went dead," I said. "I've barely had any food or sleep for nine days. I feel like a zombie and I can barely put together a thought." I had never realized that my mental functions could be so impaired. In the past, I could command my body to complete the toughest physical challenge through willpower. When Mark Burnett had asked me how I'd finished the London Marathon with a broken foot, I had said it was all in the mind. The problem, I now discovered, was that when the mind itself shut down there was no way to force it to function.

The psychologists chatted with me a while longer, then told me there was a place where I could sleep. I was shown to a tent that had a real bed and was well-stocked with food and drink. It was far from luxurious, but seemed like a castle compared to the boma.

The next morning, I was flown from the production site to the original base camp where we had received our survival training. Some of the structures, including all of the pup tents, had been removed. I stayed two nights in a rustic stone lodge, which was comfortable enough as long as I slept with mosquito netting around me. The windows were just square holes in the wall, so mosquitos and monkeys came right in. Each of the first contestants to be voted out would get to spend a couple of nights here, and then be moved out to make room for the next exile.

In a way, it was an advantage to be voted out early in the competition. The first seven outcasts were flown out of the base camp and got to travel through Kenya, staying in luxury lodges and enjoying some marvelous outings. The players eliminated during the second half of the show had to remain at the location because they would make up the jury that decided on the ultimate winner.

Mark Burnett and CBS were very generous in providing us with a wonderful vacation, and it benefited the producers as well. Legally, they couldn't have forced us to stay in Kenya if we wanted to go home, so giving us incentives to remain in the country until filming concluded was in everyone's interest.

Our entire group of seven was invited to a number of excursions and we all traveled under assumed names. I was "Joe Harris," the same alias I had been given in California. We went on a trek in which we rode camels, water skied Lake Borino and visited the Menengai Crater in the Rift

Valley. We even got to visit beautiful Diani Beach, south of Mombasa on the Indian Ocean, where we stayed at the picturesque Diani House.

The longest outing was to the Patterson Camp near the Tsavo River. The Val Kilmer movie *The Ghost and the Darkness* was based on a tragic historical event at the location: A pair of man-eating lions had killed dozens of construction workers here in 1898. Although those lions were long gone, their descendants still populated the area. On our first night, a lion killed a water buffalo fifty yards from my tent and the sound of the kill was one of the most terrifying I had ever heard. The next day we went to the dining hall and security guards wouldn't let us return to our tents. While we had been eating our lunches, the lion had returned with the rest of the pride and they were feasting on the dead buffalo. I was happy to follow the guards instructions—I had no intention of providing the lions with dessert.

There were also game drives led by local guides, which provided excellent viewing of the region's wildlife. Usually, I was the only member of the *Survivor* cast to go on these excursions, while most of the other competitors partied at the resort's swimming pool. One the main reasons I had come to Africa was to capture as much of it as I could on film, and the photographic safaris were an opportunity I couldn't pass up.

I took some remarkable photos of the region's landscape and animals, along with many pictures of Kenya's people. Despite the language barrier, I tried to communicate with them as best I could. I was impressed with their culture and their approach to life, and wish I could have conversed with them more fluently.

As much as I enjoyed my time in Africa, by the time *Survivor*'s filming wrapped up I was ready to go home. I had been apart from my family for too long. No views of Africa were as precious to me as the faces of Deborah and our children.

***

With the winner decided and the last scene filmed, all of the contestants gathered in Nairobi to catch our flights home. We were still prohibited from speaking to each other, but few of the cast seemed interested in talking anyway. Although the cameras had stopped rolling, factional differences and individual grudges remained.

We didn't fly to the United States together. The show's producers made individual travel arrangements for us so that we could each get home as quickly as possible. I had a flight to New York, where I arrived late on August 19 and spent the night at JFK's Ramada hotel. Normally, I would have told my parents that I was in the city, but the identities of the *Survivor* cast was still a tightly guarded secret. I could say nothing until the network announced the new season in early September.

The next morning, I was on board a flight to Orlando for the final leg of my odyssey. During the trip home, I reflected on my adventures and what I had gained from them. Although I didn't get far in the competition, I had achieved some of my goals: I had lost about twenty pounds, enjoyed some extraordinary experiences and taken hundreds of photographs.

But I actually came away with much more than I had ever expected, and underwent some lasting personal changes. For one thing, I learned how hunger affected your physical and mental health, and realized how undernourished people suffer terribly from its impact. I also discovered a fact that I knew, but had taken for granted: The United States is country of abundance, both in resources and in freedoms. It was eye-opening to see a third-world country where resources were scarce, opportunities limited and survival was a way of life, not a game.

I had also become more aware of how prejudices and value judgements influence the way people view each other. Whether based on age, physical appearance, nationality or gender, we all tend to make assumptions about others. Dealing with a diverse clientele in my dental practice, I had always tried to view my patients as individuals, not categories. Now I was determined to make an even stronger effort to accept everyone for whom they were and see our similarities instead of our differences.

When I arrived home, I had a few weeks to spend quiet time with my family, resume my dental work, catch up with friends and ponder the impact that the *Survivor Africa* adventure had had on me. But those days of relative normality soon came to an abrupt and shocking end.

12. The Angry Old Guy

It sure wasn't the kind of "Welcome Home" I'd been anticipating.

I had been out of the country for more than two months, with much of that time spent in fetid tents, and was eager to see our house again. When I arrived home from the Orlando airport, though, I found a manila envelope with my name on it pinned to our front door. It was a late Monday morning, Deborah was teaching and the kids were at school, so I had the house to myself. After bringing my luggage inside, I cut open the envelope to see what had been delivered in such an odd manner.

It was a letter from a supermarket tabloid giving me a preview of the next issue, with the front page headline: *Survivor Contestant is Son of Genovese Mafioso*. The author of the letter threatened to publish the story unless I agreed to do an interview about my father. Not only was that sleazy "journalism," but it was pointless. The information they cited, and the background checks that CBS had already done, were more detailed than anything I ever knew about his activities.

The big surprise to me wasn't the revelation about my father, but that the paper identified me as being on *Survivor*. Despite all the secrecy and the precautions involved in production, the identity of the contestants must have leaked out. Not knowing how to respond to the letter, I called Mark Burnett's office. He told me to ignore it, instructed me not to do any interviews and assured me that it would be handled.

I heard nothing more from the tabloid, so either Burnett or CBS must have taken care of the matter. That was the first attention I received from the media because of *Survivor*.

My reception was much warmer when the school day ended and I finally got to see my family again. They all noted the changes in my appearance; I was thinner, had grown a beard and was brown from the Kenyan sun. Deborah had changed some, too, and looked absolutely stunning. She had used my absence to make time for herself, working out with a personal trainer, eating healthier meals and getting more sleep and relaxation. Bryan and Jessica were delighted to see me again and relieved that I hadn't ended up as lion food.

While we were catching up, I learned that some suspicious activities had recently been going on. Although the identities of the *Survivor Africa* cast were supposed to be a tightly held secret, more media than that one blackmailing tabloid were on to us. *Survivor Australia* had ended its run three months earlier and had been a huge hit all over the world. Now, news hounds of every ilk were trying to dig up information about the upcoming season using methods they don't teach at the Columbia School of Journalism. Shortly before I returned home, one reporter had been going door-to-door in our neighborhood asking people if they knew anything scandalous about me; that effort continued until he knocked on the door of the homeowners association president who threw him out. Deborah even spotted well-dressed strangers going through our trash.

When I pulled into the parking lot at work for my first day back as a dentist, I immediately noticed that my home wasn't the only place under surveillance. There were actually paparazzi hiding in the bushes around my office building and snapping photos! It seemed crazy to me. What on earth could they be expecting to see—what kind of toothbrush I gave my patients? I hoped that CBS would publicly announce the cast soon. Once everything was in the open, the spy-versus-spy games should cease.

In early September, the network unveiled its fall television schedule. The cast of *Survivor Africa* was revealed and episodes were slated to begin airing in a couple of weeks. Nationally, there was a lot of excitement about the show as a whole. Locally, there was strong interest in the two Orlando area contestants, Jessie Camacho and myself.

Then, the terrorist attacks of September 11 changed the world in a single day of pure horror. Shock, anger and sorrow enveloped the country and normal activities were put on hold as we all tried to cope with the enormity of the tragedy.

***

Gradually, as Americans struggled to get back to enjoying the small things that give life flavor, we learned that we could still laugh at a joke, sing a love song or enjoy a ballgame. Late-night talk shows resumed production, baseball season picked up again with the Yankees making it into in the World Series and the premiere of *Survivor* was given a new air date in October.

An increasing amount of media attention in Orlando was given to its hometown contestants. I was already known to a number of television and radio hosts through my affiliation with the Orlando Magic and my charitable work, and received numerous requests for interviews and appearances. I also did some joint events with Jessie, one of which was an autograph signing and a prize giveaway at a Magic game.

Deborah was interviewed by a newspaper reporter who asked if my time in Africa had changed me. She answered that what struck her most was that I was now very conscientious about conserving water and other resources. I had seen how the people of Kenya wasted nothing of the little they had, and I thought theirs was an example worth following.

Nationally, the cast was featured in magazines such as *People* and *Us Weekly*. For the first time, the same issue of *TV Guide* was published with sixteen different covers, one picturing each of the *Survivor* contestants.

Although I received a lot of attention from strangers about the show, I heard almost nothing from my parents or siblings. The only one to call me was my brother Anthony, who had been struggling to start an acting career. He complained that I only went on *Survivor* to make him jealous, and he reminded me quite emphatically that he was the true actor in the family.

The first episode of *Survivor Africa* finally aired on Thursday, October 11. Deborah surprised me by throwing a spectacular watch party at our home. We had two hundred guests, half wearing red headbands for Samburu and the other half wearing yellow for the Boran tribe. A tiki hut was set up in our backyard to serve drinks, and topiaries of African animals were placed around the lawn. The phenomenal percussionist Robert Thomas Jr., who played with Santana, Branford Marsalis and Stan Getz, was there with his gear and he drummed along with the *Survivor* theme. Of course, no one—including Deborah—knew that I would only be on for two more episodes. I had never revealed anything about the eliminations. We all had a great time and ended the night thoroughly exhausted.

The next morning, Deborah and I had to force ourselves to get up early and go to the airport. We were headed to New York, where I promptly got myself in trouble again.

***

One day, while we were sitting around starving in our boma, the forty-somethings of the Samburu tribe—Frank, Linda, T-Bird and myself—were talking about the foods we missed most. Of course, thinking about tasty meals only makes the torture worse, but, when you're hungry, food is about the only thing on your mind. I made the comment that as soon as I got back to the States I was going to fly to New Jersey and have chicken marsala and calamari at Luciano's. Frank said that he didn't know what those were—his experience with Italian food was limited to spaghetti and meatballs.

A thought popped into my head, and, as many of them do, it immediately emerged from my mouth. "When we get back," I suggested, "let's all four of us get together for dinner at Luciano's. I guarantee it'll be the best Italian food you've ever eaten."

They all liked the idea and we agreed to set a date. When I got home to Orlando and told Deborah about the plan, she said that it was impolite to invite only some of the cast and not the others. Since I had everyone's email, I contacted all sixteen to ask if they wanted to get together for a reunion dinner in New Jersey, and all but a few agreed. However, I didn't think to clear it with CBS.

The network didn't learn of our plans until the day of the dinner. Diane had been voted off in the season premiere and, like all the contestants, was scheduled to do media appearances the day after her elimination. She was assigned a limousine to take her to her appointments during the day and was permitted to keep it for personal use until late that night. One of the CBS publicists accompanying Diane asked what she wanted to do after the media tour. She replied, "I'm having dinner with Doc and the crew in Bayonne." That piece of information was quickly passed up the network's chain of command.

Deborah and I had checked into the Hilton in Times Square, still tired from the watch party the night before. It had been a challenge getting to the hotel because there had just been an anthrax attack at NBC News and some transportation was shut down.

I was about to take a short nap, when an executive from CBS telephoned our room. She was cordial but emphatic. "You *have* to cancel this dinner tonight."

"I'm not canceling anything," I said.

"Didn't you read your contract?"

"Uh, no." Reading a ninety-page contract had never made it to the top of my to-do list.

"You are not allowed to be together with the other contestants until the last episode has aired. What if you're seen? There are reporters and paparazzi *everywhere*." Her anxiety was audible.

I hadn't meant to cause anyone distress, but couldn't renege on my invitation. "I'm sorry, but I invited these people a long time ago and they've already been coming into town. I can't cancel it now." She began to protest, and I went on, "I *guarantee* there will be no problems with the media. We will be completely shielded from them." Luciano's had some customers who were very particular about security and discretion. In fact, while I was still in Africa, my father had held his traditional just-released-from-prison celebration in the same restaurant.

"Are you sure?" the exasperated woman asked.

"There's even going to be FBI there," I said. "We'll be well protected and *nobody's* coming near us."

"*FBI?*"

"Look, why don't you join us at the dinner and you'll see for yourself that there won't be any trouble—and you'll have a great meal."

That evening, two black limousines drove into the working class city of Bayonne and pulled up to the curb in front of Luciano's. One of the limos was Diane's; she had kindly invited Deborah and me to join her in the ride from New York. The other car carried two CBS executives who had come to monitor the proceedings.

One of the network people was the nervous woman I had spoken to on the phone. When we got out of our cars, she came over and introduced herself. She glanced up and down the street, an expression of distaste on her face and clearly ill at ease. Bayonne was not the Upper East Side of

Manhattan, and Luciano's wasn't the kind of restaurant that offered a finger bowl.

As we all started walking toward the door, the CBS woman pulled up short. Two brawny young men in muscle shirts, each sporting black pompadours, stood outside with their arms folded across their chests. "Who are they?" she whispered to me.

"Those are the FBI I told you about: Full-Blooded Italians."

She gasped and appeared about to faint. I gave a nod to the young men and ushered everyone past them into the restaurant.

Luciano himself led us upstairs to a private room that was reserved for special occasions. Soon the rest of the guests arrived—about thirteen of the sixteen contestants were able to make it—and we began eating. We ate family-style from magnificent platters piled with the restaurant's finest foods and enjoyed a delightful reunion.

Initially, the two CBS executives tried to listen to everything anyone said. Although their concern about paparazzi was alleviated, they were still worried that the results of the competition might be revealed. The first seven of us to be voted out still had no idea who won, and we were dining with players who had been on the jury and knew the outcome. But none of us discussed the game at the dinner. We all talked about what an adventure Africa had been, how great it was to see our families again and what a surprise all the publicity was turning out to be.

Even the network people relaxed after a while, and they began to share in the fun and the camaraderie. And everyone agreed: It was the best Italian food they had ever tasted.

***

In real time, *Survivor* eliminations took place every three days of the competition. In television time, it was once per weekly episode. So, two weeks after Diane was voted out in the premiere, my farewell show was aired. The next morning, as the latest contestant to leave the contest, I was launched on my week of public appearances.

It began, as it did for every contestant, at CBS Studios in New York. I spent all of Friday morning on live radio, being interviewed by various hosts and answering fans' call-in questions for CBS affiliates throughout the country. One of those who got through claimed to be Steve Martin and said that I must be real sadist to be a dentist. I assumed the caller was some joker referencing Martin's role as the sadistic dentist in *Little Shop of Horrors*. I answered, "Yeah, and I'd like to give *you* a root canal." The next day, we learned that the caller really was Steve Martin and that he really hated dentists!

My first television appearance was on *Live! with Regis and Kelly*. I followed First Lady Laura Bush, but wasn't able to meet her. Secret Service protection was extremely tight and she was taken off the set with a cordon of security around her.

When I took my seat, the first thing Kelly Ripa said to me was, "I have to ask you this question, Doc: Why do dentists have the highest suicide rate?"

"How would I know?" I quipped. "I'm still alive!"

She laughed.

Then I gave her an explanation. "Our profession isn't especially popular—who *likes* to go to the dentist? Usually somebody comes to us in pain and fear. They walk into an exam room that smells like a hospital and is full of sharp instruments. We take out a ginormous needle and jab your gum, then we pry your jaw open and poke and drill for a while. You can't talk, you're drooling and you know you're going to be in pain when the anesthetic wears off. And after all that, you have to go to the front desk to pay for the lovely time you just had. So people don't like us. We're probably less popular than baseball umpires."

"You are a funny man," she said, although it was one of my more serious answers.

Soon after my morning chat with Regis and Kelly, the network flew me to California for *The Late Late Show* with Craig Kilborn. I remembered him from his time anchoring ESPN's *SportsCenter*.

While I was waiting my turn to go on, Bob Saget came off the set. When he saw me, he said, "Dr. B! Are you happy to be on the show tonight?"

"No, not really," I answered honestly.

Saget did a double take. "Huh?"

"I'd rather be at Yankee Stadium. I got tickets to the World Series game tonight and I'm gonna miss it." As the first World Series game in New York after 9/11, it promised to be a major event, with President Bush throwing out the ceremonial first pitch and the entire city displaying its pride as New Yorkers and Americans.

Although it couldn't compete with the World Series, I thoroughly enjoyed my appearance with Kilborn. He had a young audience, a lot of them in college, and they had wonderful energy and enthusiasm. I was delighted that Kilborn showcased my photographic work in addition to speaking about my *Survivor* stint. He displayed some of my photos on camera, most of them action shots that I'd taken during sporting events.

After taping the show, I caught the next flight I could get for New York. When the Yankees took the field the following night, I was in the stands and watched them pull out a 4-3 win on a Derek Jeter extra-inning home run.

Although it wasn't required of me, I agreed to do a couple of radio shows with some "shock jocks." The CBS publicist forewarned me that I was known as "the angry old guy" and that they might want to go after me for that.

"I wasn't angry," I said, rather puzzled.

"No, but every contestant has a persona so they can be easily identified, and you're 'the angry old guy.'"

"I can handle myself," I told the publicist, and went ahead with the shows. I never minded being kidded and I knew that I could give it right back.

The first show was Howard Stern, and he began with a typical Howard question, asking whether Jessie and I had sex in Africa.

"Are you nuts?" I answered. "She's young enough to be my daughter!"

"That doesn't matter," said Stern.

"Look, I've been happily married for more than twenty years and I have a hot wife."

He leered. "Well, maybe we should bring her out here!"

Oh crap, I thought. Deborah was waiting for me in the green room with the publicist from CBS. If Stern brought Deborah out and said something inappropriate to her, I would have to hit him.

Maybe he noticed something in my expression. For whatever reason, Stern switched topics completely, asking me what I thought of his sidekick Baba Booey's teeth.

Somebody brought me a pair of latex gloves and I did a quick exam. "They're terrible," I said. "The crowns are too big and overly contoured." I said to the young man, "I'll tell you what: You fly down to Winter Park and I'll do your teeth for free just so you can see what good dental work can look like."

They all laughed appreciatively, and Stern was very respectful for the rest of the show. One of the things he wanted to know was whether the lions on the program were fake—he thought they sounded like Disney characters. I assured him they were genuine and a real danger.

Howard Stern was Mr. Rogers compared to Opie and Anthony. The CBS publicist warned me that the two hosts were planning to tear me to shreds. I went on anyway, and started joking around as soon as I got in the studio. That seemed to disarm them and we had a fun show.

My *Survivor* publicity tour came to an end on Thursday, November first, when the next episode aired and Linda—one of my fellow forty-somethings in Samburu—was exiled. I had enjoyed my week in the spotlight, but was happy to pass it on to Linda. I didn't even watch the program that evening because I was happily in my seat at Yankee Stadium watching my team win a twelve-inning World Series thriller.

***

Episodes of *Survivor Africa* continued to air from October through to the finale in January. In November, the *Australian Outback* season won an Emmy award as television's "Outstanding Non-Fiction Program" for 2001. Our season proved not to be as popular at the previous one, however. Viewership had dropped to two-thirds of what it had been for the Australia entry and reviews were lukewarm. The lack of food during filming had simply made us too sluggish to be exciting.

Public interest picked up for the finale on January 10. I participated in the reunion episode hosted by Bryant Gumbel on the same day. It was the first time that the cast was all together again. When we were backstage, we didn't say much about what had transpired during filming. It was clear that there were still hard feelings between some of the cast, but no confrontations. A lot of the younger contestants talked about how they were looking for agents and trying to parlay their *Survivor* fame into acting or modeling careers.

The next month, *Survivor Marquesas* premiered and the national spotlight shifted to the new season and the new cast. To my surprise, I still got some attention—and in unexpected ways.

When baseball season began, I received a phone call from a friend of mine who had been at Yankee Stadium that day. A picture of me wearing a Yankees cap and my *Survivor* outfit was shown on the scoreboard with the words: "This person participated in the hit show Survivor. What is his occupation?" My friend yelled out, "That's Dr. B! He's my dentist!"

I had packed the baseball cap for my Africa adventure hoping that I could wear it on the show. Just before the game began, Mark Burnett and his assistant came to each of our tents to inspect the clothing that we would be bringing with us into camp. Burnett said that I couldn't wear the hat until they were able to clear it with Major League Baseball and the New York Yankees. Fortunately, permission came quickly and I was able to show my Yankee pride. In the back of my mind, I had hoped that by wearing the cap on national television, the ball club might invite me to a game. Instead, my picture turned up as a trivia question!

Although I never saw it, I heard from a number of people over the years that I was also the subject of a trivia question on MTV. The question was, "Who was 'The Angry Old Guy' on *Survivor*?"

***

Less than two months after the *Survivor Africa* reunion show, my father was arrested again. Although I had made the cover of *TV Guide*, Carlo Bilancione made headlines in the *New York Times*. He was one of seven "Genovese crime family associates" rounded up in a government crackdown on corruption in the longshoremen's union. This time, he didn't call to tell me of the arrest and no one in my family ever said a word to me about it. In fact, I didn't learn of his latest legal trouble until much later, and the only information I could obtain was from the published record.

About half a dozen federal and state law enforcement agencies had collaborated in "Operation Shout," targeting Local No. 1588 of the International Longshoreman's Association. That was the Bayonne local where my father had once been field boss. He was charged with racketeering, theft by extortion, commercial bribery, and conspiracy. The actual criminal enterprise that was alleged by the government was that my father and his codefendants required workers to pay them for job assignments, promotions and overtime.

According to the New Jersey Attorney General, the investigation had been active since October 2000, and video surveillance equipment had been planted in the union office to record activities and conversations. When law enforcement realized that wires to the recording device had been discovered, they hurried to make the arrests while a grand jury was still considering indictments. All seven men were taken into custody in early morning raids, and all without incident. The judge entered a "not guilty" plea on my father's behalf, and released him on $150,000 bail.

My father made the *Times* again in May when the indictments were handed down. The counts against him had been increased to eight.

Then, as far as I know, nothing more happened with his case. I don't think my father served any additional prison time. His employment registration with the Waterfront Commission had already been revoked because of his previous conviction, and perhaps the authorities were satisfied with that. In any event, the federal government took over running Local No. 1588 through a court-appointed trustee. The man chosen for that task was Robert J. McGuire, who had been New York City Police Commissioner under Ed Koch. McGuire was in, and my father and his friends were out.

***

Although national attention had died down for me, I received a lot of invitations for appearances in Florida. I had already been active in the community for years, and *Survivor* provided some new opportunities.

One day, I received a phone call from Scott duPont, a well-known actor, producer, and director. He was calling on behalf of the Florida Motion Picture and Television Association which was holding its annual Crystal Reel Awards show in June. There would be a banquet at Disney's posh Swan and Dolphin hotel, with celebrity guests and a televised awards ceremony. Scott said that since I was known for my photography as well as *Survivor*, he hoped that I would present the Crystal Reel Award for photography. Deborah was invited as well, of course, and I happily agreed.

The event was red carpet, black tie and first class all the way. Burt Reynolds was there to receive a Lifetime Achievement Award for his many years promoting film and theater in Florida. Other celebrities in attendance, almost all with a Florida connection, included Lee Majors, Oscar nominee Andy Garcia and Johnny Martino, who'd had an iconic role as Paulie in *The Godfather*. I spoke with Martino that evening and it turned out that we were distant cousins. The hosts for the event were Kirsten Storms, an Orlando native starring in the soap opera *Days of Our Lives*, and David Faustino, best known for his Bud Bundy character on *Married with Children*.

The awards ceremony began, and when it came time for me to present the photography award, I was introduced by David Faustino. He mispronounced my name as "Carl Babaloney."

I walked up on stage, but instead of going to the lectern I went over to Faustino who had stepped back to give me room at the microphone. I flashed him some Neapolitan hand gestures and said, "Faustino—that's Italian right?"

He nodded.

"And you can't pronounce an Italian name? Say Ma-ca-ro-ni."

Looking rather sheepish, he repeated "Ma-ca-ro-ni."

"Now say Bi-lan-ci-o-ne."

"Bi-lan-ci-o-ne."

"Good. *That's* who I am."

As the guest of honor, Burt Reynolds was seated in the front row with his entourage. When I turned to face the audience, I saw that he and his friends were roaring with laughter, as was most of the rest of the crowd.

After presenting the award, I returned to my seat next to Deborah. She was mortified by what I had done. I don't think anyone else minded. Sometimes the unexpected can help liven things up, especially at an awards show.

When the ceremony ended, a meticulously dressed woman of about fifty approached me. "Are you really a dentist?" she asked.

I assured her that I was, and wondered if she was going to ask me to check her teeth.

"You should be on television," she gushed. "I *love* your energy and your personality. Can I represent you?

"Represent me?"

"Yes, I'm a talent agent."

She handed me her card, and I gave her my phone number.

I had been to enough social events in my life to know that ideas and proposals discussed at parties are usually mere idle chatter, so I didn't believe anything would come of her offer. I turned out to be mistaken. *Survivor* would not be my final appearance before a camera.

13. Giving Back

Brief as it was, my appearance on *Survivor Africa* opened unexpected doors for me that led to some fascinating new ventures. More importantly, it provided me with a number of opportunities to help people facing serious life challenges.

When I returned from the competition, I was asked if I was happy to get back to a normal life again. My answer was that I never felt *abnormal*—the show was simply another adventure for me to experience and I was always adventurous. Moreover, I was now able to use whatever renown I had to benefit other people.

I had been very fortunate in my life and always believed that it was important to share and to help others. But I didn't really know what charities most deserved support or how best to contribute. I usually didn't became active in a cause until I had a personal connection to someone facing a hardship.

In the 1990s, my mother-in-law was stricken with breast cancer, a disease that had taken the lives of several women in my wife's family. I ran the 1994 New York Marathon on behalf of the Susan G. Komen Breast Cancer Foundation, as it was then called, to help raise funds for the organization.

When I learned that my long-time dental hygienist's husband was suffering from debilitating diabetes, I contacted the American Diabetes Association to see what I could do. I organized a group of friends and we worked to raise money and awareness. Our group was able to raise about fifty thousand dollars, all of which went to the ADA for research and treatments. It was for the ADA that I ran the 1999 London Marathon.

What I discovered after being on national television was that I now had a broader platform and more ways that I could contribute to a range of worthy causes. In addition to my individual efforts, I could help draw media attention to the issue and enlist other figures from sports and television to lend their names and time as well.

I no longer limited myself to causes that involved people close to me. Once my name was revealed as a *Survivor* contestant, I received numerous letters and phone calls from various charities asking for my assistance. I had never realized that there were so many different struggles faced by so many people. As I began to learn more about these issues, I determined to use whatever public recognition I had to make others aware of them, too.

***

Not long after the *Survivor Africa* finale aired, I received a phone call requesting my participation in a fashion show. I knew as much about fashion shows as I did about astrophysics, but I wasn't wanted for my sartorial expertise. The organizers of the show asked if they could promote my appearance and use my name to attract more people to the event. When I learned that the fashion show was to benefit a local women's shelter, I said I would be happy to help.

Lisa Merlin House, in the Pine Hills neighborhood of Orlando, was a last refuge for women who had no place else to go. Many were victims of domestic abuse, some had substance abuse problems and all were desperately in need of a safe, supportive environment.

I promptly contacted every one of the contestants who had been with me in Africa, trying to recruit them to join me. I figured if my name would help get attention, then having more of the cast involved should get more attention. The response was amazing—fifteen of them, including winner Ethan Zohn and runner-up Kim Johnson, agreed to come to Orlando to participate in the fashion show.

On the day before the event, all of us visited Lisa Merlin House to meet the residents and hear their stories. Much of what we saw and heard was heartbreaking, but it was also inspiring to see how determined these women were to rebuild their lives. And it unified the cast; there were no rivalries, no schemes, no grudges. We were all going to pull together to help others.

The fashion show, held at the Downtown Orlando Marriott, was well-attended and a lot of fun. It was broadcast on the local CBS affiliate and hosted by the station's news anchors. In addition to the *Survivor* cast, participants included Florida first lady Columba Bush, basketball stars Katie Douglas and Nykesha Sales of the WNBA's Orlando Miracle, as well as a couple of women who excelled at pageants: Miss Florida Kelli Meierhenry and former Mrs. Florida Jackie Siegel, later known as "The Queen of Versailles."

People bought tickets for a dinner and the fashion show, there was a silent auction and a raffle was held. All members of the *Survivor* cast participated as models, as did Deborah, Jessica and Bryan. It was a tremendous success, with a great deal of money raised and a lot of local publicity was generated for Lisa Merlin House. I was glad that I had been able to contribute, although I don't think I made much of an impression on the catwalk—not a single modeling agent asked to represent me.

***

My fellow cast members had come to Orlando when I called on them, and I was happy to travel to their charitable events when they asked me. We had learned how much we could accomplish when we joined together in a cause.

A couple of months after the fashion show, I got a phone call from Diane Ogden, who had shared her limo with Deborah and me for that dinner at Luciano's. I always liked Diane, who had a big heart and an easy-going manner. Her audition video for *Survivor* was about as serious as mine: She held a cigarette in one hand, a cup of coffee in the other, and basically dared the producers to choose her for the cast.

After *Survivor*, Diane had returned to her job as a mail carrier in Lincoln, Nebraska, and was considered a hometown hero as the first Nebraskan to take on the *Survivor* challenge. Then she did something for the community that was truly heroic.

Camp Kindle was founded in Nebraska as a summer camp for children impacted by AIDS and HIV. The camp welcomed youngsters from throughout the Midwest and provided them with recreational and therapeutic activities in a supportive environment. Diane was active in her son's scouting troop and familiar with camping. She got together with the founder of Camp Kindle to see how she could assist the program. What Diane came up with was "SurvivorFest," bringing together members of every season of *Survivor* to raise money for the camp.

In July 2002, for the first time, contestants from all four *Survivor* seasons teamed up for charity. More than thirty participated, with eleven from *Survivor Africa*, as well as Rudy Boesch, Boston Rob Mariano, Jerri Manthey and Jenna Lewis among the representatives from other seasons.

Having been in the Navy, I was especially happy to meet Rudy, who was a legend in the service. He had been an underwater demolition frogman, one of the first Navy SEALs and the longest-serving SEAL ever. He was awarded a Bronze Star for heroism in the Vietnam War and a Defense Superior Service Medal upon his retirement after forty-five years of active military duty. The two of us hit it off and spoke for some time. He was gruff, blunt and politically incorrect. I thoroughly enjoyed listening to what this wise old veteran had to say.

We spent several days in Nebraska, meeting the Camp Kindle children and publicizing the fundraising events. The was a dinner, games, an auction of *Survivor* memorabilia and a dance. The SurvivorFest finale was held in the Pershing Center, an auditorium that held more than four thousand people. Fans bought tickets to see us and the place was packed.

I was amazed at how many people recognized our faces and knew our stories. But I suppose it was to be expected, since we had appeared in their living rooms and bedrooms quite often. *Survivor* had been on television every week for four months, with tens of millions of viewers. After being voted out, the name and picture of each contestant was still shown in the opening montage. Even years later, we were still being recognized by people we had never met.

Thanks to Diane, the event was a great success. With the money we raised and the publicity we garnered, Camp Kindle was able to expand and provide services to more children. Just as in Orlando, there were no egos or conflicts among the contestants; we all knew when the game was over and serious work needed to be done.

***

The next month, I was in another charity event in Orlando. This was the second annual "T-Mac Bowl" to benefit the Boggy Creek Camp for children with serious illnesses. The camp is located not far from Orlando, and provides children with fishing, horseback riding, swimming, boating and numerous other activities. The event was organized by Orlando Magic all-star Tracy McGrady.

I'd known Tracy for years, he was a patient of mine, and he was an accomplished bowler as well as one of the top basketball players in the country. He thought my recent *Survivor* fame might bring some added publicity to the event, so I was asked to join as one of the celebrity bowlers. Naturally, I agreed.

Most of those participating were well-known professional athletes. In addition to T-Mac, there were other Magic players I knew well, such as Shaquille O'Neal and Doc Rivers, along with many NBA and NFL stars. I couldn't compete with any of them on the basketball court or the football field, but I figured I could hold my own in bowling.

On Sunday afternoon, I showed up at the Dowdy Pavilion World Bowling Center in Orlando, and learned that I was assigned the lane next to Shaq. He spotted me carrying my own bowling bag and shoes. "Hey, Doc, you're a bowler?" he asked.

"For years," I said. Where I grew up, nobody went to play golf at a country club. The bowling alley is where working men went.

"You any good?"

"Well, I was on a bowling team in the Navy and we won the Commander's Cup." My naval experience had clearly been very different from Rudy Boesch's.

"What's your average?"

"One ninety-five." I was feeling competitive with all the professional athletes around and was hoping to break two hundred this day.

I ended up beating Shaq's score by a large margin, but he certainly got more style points. He was seven-foot-one, about three hundred pounds, and wore a size-22 sneaker. His fingers were the diameter of bratwurst and there was no bowling ball with holes large enough to accommodate him. Shaq simply wrapped his hand around the bowling ball as easily as I could grip a softball and launched it down the lane. The impact was so hard, it sounded as if the pins would shatter.

The fundraising target for the event was $100,000. Between the admission price people had paid to watch us bowl, and the auction of autographed memorabilia, I believe that goal was achieved. And, once again, everyone had a great time pulling together to help children.

***

By the time the eighth season of *Survivor* aired, I assumed the cast of *Survivor Africa* would be old news and largely forgotten. I was very happy to learn that my help was still sought for charitable events and that I could still contribute.

In April 2004, I was invited to play in a celebrity softball game by Mike Nunez, an executive with Junior Achievement of East Central Florida. Junior Achievement is a nonprofit organization that helps prepare young people to enter the workplace by providing them with essential skills and experience. My response was an immediate, "I'll be there."

When Mike told me the names of some of the other players, I felt like I'd be going into a sports fan's dream. The roster included former major league baseball players Sudden Sam McDowell, Tim "Rock" Raines and Lee Stange. Football stars Hershel Walker, Mercury Morris and Leonard Marshall were slated to attend. There would be hockey players, professional wrestlers, a couple of pro surfers and some nonathletes such as model Kim Alexis and *Dance Fever* host Denny Terrio—and me.

As excited as I was, my petite, quiet, devout seventy-year-old mother was even more so. That's because she was absolutely crazy about professional wrestling. Friends knew not to call the house on a Friday night because she would be riveted to the television, watching the latest offering from the World Wrestling Federation. My mother had an exquisite China cabinet where she displayed delicate teacups, commemorative plates and various porcelain knick-knacks. In a place of honor on the top shelf of that cabinet was one of her proudest possessions, a foot-long two-by-four piece of pine signed "To Vivian, Your Friend, Hacksaw Jim Duggan." Duggan was a wrestler whose trademark was hitting opponents in the head with a two-by-four; I had met him and got him to sign the piece of wood for her. My mother was determined to witness the softball game—actually to see the wrestlers—and she talked my father into scheduling their next visit to coincide with the event.

When we all got to Space Coast Stadium, home of the minor league Brevard Manatees in Rockledge, my family made their way to the grandstand and I went to the locker room. The first person I saw was Herschel Walker. He looked at me and said, "Hey, you're Doc B!"

I was stunned. A Heisman Trophy winner recognized *me*?

Walker went on, "You got robbed on that *Survivor* show."

"Oh, no. I should have done better," I said, still staring at him in awe. Finally, I blurted, "*You're* Herschel Walker!"

He smiled, and held out a pen and a softball. "Would you mind signing this for my son?"

I was happy to, but so flabbergasted that Herschel Walker was asking for *my* autograph that I probably misspelled my name. He then returned the favor, signing several items for me. As he did, I commented, "You look like you could still be playing football—you work out a lot?"

"Just ballet and yoga."

"Seriously?"

"Oh yes. Those keep the muscles flexible. I don't do any weight training."

We were to be teammates in today's game, and I asked him what position he was playing.

"Catcher. How about you?"

"Left field." The assignments didn't make sense to me. I was a dentist and Herschel was an athlete—he should be playing outfield and I should be stuck behind the plate. Mike Nunez was approaching and I asked him if we could trade positions. He agreed, and it was a good thing we made the change because Herschel ran down some long fly balls that I would have merely waved at.

Nunez had actually come over to tell me about some schtick he had planned for the game. While I put on my uniform, he said, "George Steele is coaching in the third base dugout. If you get on base today and make it to third, he's going to run out and pretend to hit you with a chair. Are you okay with that?"

George "The Animal" Steele was one of my mother's favorite wrestlers and an occasional actor who had played Tor Johnson in the Johnny Depp movie *Ed Wood*. He was a hirsute giant whose ring persona was that of a wild man. I thought Mike's idea sounded like fun. After all, people were coming to the game for entertainment, not a serious baseball contest.

As our team got ready, I also had some great conversations with Sam McDowell and Tim Raines. Both of them were very down to earth and happy to talk baseball.

The game got underway before a packed crowd. Tickets had been offered a month ahead of time and sales had been excellent. I saw my mother and the rest of my family in their seats and could tell they were having a blast.

A couple of innings into the game, I managed to hit a long drive and leg out a double. Playing among all those real athletes, I think it was one of my proudest moments in sports. I was so happy, that when the next batter moved me over to third I forgot what was about to happen.

Out of the third base dugout came George Steele, a bald-headed monster of a man, roaring at the top of his lungs and waving a chair over his head. Apparently, he had forgotten something too—the fact that he was only supposed to *pretend* to hit me.

The chair made full impact with my skull and I saw stars. He raised it again, and I started running out toward left field to get away from him. The fans were laughing, Steele was roaring and my mother was cheering him on!

When the game was over, I went over to my mother. She had a big smile on her face and she told me what fun it had been to watch Steele chasing me around the ballpark.

"Maybe it was fun for you," I said, "but he really hit me with that chair. It *hurt*!"

"Oh, don't be a baby," she said.

***

About two years later, Mike Nunez called me again. He had an idea for starting a new charitable organization and wanted to know if I thought it was feasible.

Mike's plan was to organize a group called Hearts of Reality. Instead of initiating contacts with random reality stars every time there was an event coming up, Hearts of Reality would maintain a roster of reality veterans who were willing to participate on a regular basis. The charity that Hearts of Reality would support was Give Kids the World Village in Kissimmee, Florida.

Give Kids the World was founded by Henri Landwirth, a holocaust survivor who had lost both parents and five years of his youth in Nazi concentration camps including Auschwitz. He became a successful hotel owner in Florida and a philanthropist dedicated to helping children. The village, designed like a Candyland theme park with charming venues and colorful villas, serves children with critical and terminal illnesses. The kids and their families are provided a week-long, all-expenses-paid vacation. During that week, the families get some much-deserved relaxation. They visit Disney and SeaWorld, and the kids have the kind of fun that all children should be able to enjoy.

Mike asked me, "Do you think something like Hearts of Reality could work?"

"I have no idea," I answered. "But I'm in. Let's give it a go and find out."

It took off beyond anything we could have imagined. I contacted people I knew from my season, and enlisted about half a dozen for the new venture. The roster grew quickly thereafter. Initially, participants were mostly from *Survivor*, but later expanded to include contestants from *Big Brother*, *The Amazing Race* and other reality TV shows. Hearts of

Reality now has about 150 participants. I've remained active with the organization and committed to its objectives.

Part of the purpose of Hearts of Reality is to raise funds, of course. Over the years, this has been accomplished in a number of ways. There are ongoing eBay auctions of autographed photos and other memorabilia. Individual members of Hearts of Reality each try to raise a certain amount of money for the charity, and fans can contribute to a specific player's goal on the organization's website. Some reality stars auction a Zoom meeting, in which a fan with the winning bid can speak with them personally. I've auctioned photo excursions, in which I would take the winning bidder on a half-day photography outing; I provided the equipment, guidance and lunch.

In December, the in-person activities are held and continue for several days. There's a party hosted by *People* magazine, a day of autograph signing, auctions, a dinner and dances. For several years, fans could pay to join us on a Victory casino cruise. I did one of these in 2018 with Joey Fatone, former singer with NSYNC and a veteran of many television programs including *Family Feud* and *Dancing with the Stars*. He lived in the Orlando area, too, and was also very active with children's charities.

The highlight every year at Give Kids the World Village is the party that we throw for the children and their parents. This is geared entirely for the enjoyment of the kids. Young children don't watch *Big Brother* or *Survivor* and have no idea who we are. So we dispense with the celebrity role and simply entertain them. We'd usually come to the party dressed as characters—pirates and princesses and superheroes—hand out some small gifts and spend a little time with the kids and their families.

One year, I was dressed as a pirate with big fake teeth. As I was going around the room, I noticed a small, thin boy of about four or five who seemed rather withdrawn. His name was Connor and he was with his family from Ohio. Connor's father told me that this trip was the first time his son had been out of the hospital in his life. Give Kids the World provided complete medical care and equipment to meet each child's particular needs, freeing them as much as possible from the confines of a hospital setting.

I tried to talk with Connor, but he remained very shy. So I began speaking to him in a Donald Duck voice and his face lit up. I played with him for a while, keeping up the funny voice, and he was clearly having a fun time. Then I moved on to meet with some of the other children.

The next December, at the orientation session that takes place when families first arrive, I saw a man of about thirty walk onto the stage and I remembered him as Connor's father. As he stepped to the microphone, Connor's picture was projected on the screen. The boy had died during the past year.

Connor's father proceeded to tell us what a profound impact their week at the Village had had on Connor and his entire family. He said that Connor's two brothers sometimes felt neglected because one of their parents was always at the hospital with Connor. When they were at the Village and saw all of the other ill children, they realized how fortunate they really were and understood the challenges that these courageous kids face. Because of the positive impact Give

Kids the World had had on them, Connor's parents quit their jobs in Ohio, moved the family to Orlando where they found new employment, and now volunteered at the Village so that they could assist others the way they had been helped.

Hearing him speak, and remembering Connor, I was choked up and struggling not to openly cry. I thought of Connor's star that would remain in the Village. Each child is given a personalized golden star when they arrive and it is hung from the ceiling in the Castle of Miracles. Connor's is one of 130,000 still sparkling there.

There was a break after Connor's father spoke and I went over to express my sympathy for the loss of his son.

"You're the pirate!" he said. "Connor loved your Donald Duck voice. And you really made him happy—he kept telling us that one of the highlights of his time here was meeting 'the pirate that talked like Donald Duck.'"

I was surprised and overwhelmed to hear that I'd had such an impact on the boy. Once again, I had to fight back tears. I chatted a short time longer with Connor's father, then excused myself before I started crying aloud.

In the game *Survivor* there are "reward challenges." In real life, I've found that there is nothing more rewarding than being able to bring some happiness to a child such as Connor.

14. Into the Wild

Childhood experiences and early impressions often establish the directions for some of the paths we take later in life. When I was growing up in Brooklyn, I enjoyed watching *Mutual of Omaha's Wild Kingdom* on television, fascinated by the exotic animals from all over the world. I also liked looking up at the planes from JFK and LaGuardia airports flying over the city, and dreamed of places I might visit. I was determined to travel someday and see in person the wonders that planet Earth has to offer—the people, the wildlife and the environment.

It was years before I could realize this goal and "someday" seemed a long way off. Serving in the Navy, building a dental practice and raising a family didn't allow time for extended vacations. Eventually, it became possible to travel and I tried to see as much of the world as time and money would permit. And with my camera, I could preserve not only memories, but images of the natural world that were fast disappearing.

***

In 1995, when we were finally able to take a family trip, we traveled all the way to the other side of the globe. Deborah and I, along with eleven-year-old Jessica, eight-year-old Bryan and Deborah's parents, embarked on a two-week visit to Australia. Instead of booking a tour, we stayed in a hotel in Sydney and made it our home base. We then set our own itinerary so that we could pursue activities that would satisfy everyone's interests.

One of the first places I wanted to visit in Sydney was the Taronga Zoo. It was on the north shore of Sydney Harbor, with a view of the Sydney Opera House across the water. Since its opening in 1916, the zoo had become world famous for providing the animals with natural environments and maintaining strong conservation and education programs.

On a warm sunny day, we all went to the zoo and it was just as beautiful as I had heard. And, of course, it featured animals that existed on no other continent in the world. I was lugging my ever-present camera so that I could photograph these unique, beautiful creatures.

We were all walking together through the zoo, when I was captivated by an adorable koala napping in a eucalyptus tree. I wanted to take his photo, but his face was turned away from me. I waited patiently, assuming that he would have to wake up and shift his position soon. When he didn't, I asked a nearby zookeeper, "Does he just sleep all day?"

"Pretty much," she answered.

"How do I get him to look at me so I can take his picture?"

She laughed. "It doesn't work that way."

I told my family to continue through the zoo without me because I was going to stay a while. They were accustomed to me taking time for photos, so they went off, contentedly eating ice creams on their way to the platypus exhibit.

My estimate of "a while" turned out to be two hours. I stood patiently, my camera at the ready, waiting for the koala to cooperate. The zookeeper seemed to think I was nuts, but I had a gut feeling that my determination would pay off. Suddenly, the koala woke up and turned his face to me. I snapped three quick shots before he lowered his head and dozed off again.

When we got back from the trip and I had the photos developed, I saw that the shots of that drowsy koala really were something special. I entered one of them in a contest, and it ended up being published in a book! That was the first photograph of mine to be published anywhere.

I had another first at the Great Barrier Reef. My father-in-law Henry had been giving me technical advice on photography for more than ten years. By this time, he didn't do much photography himself anymore but continued to mentor me. For the trip, he had lent me his large Nikonos camera rig so that I could try my hand at underwater photography.

Deborah and I went out on a dive boat from Cairns in Queensland, which took us to the Saxon and Norman reefs northeast of Cairns. The dive master was excellent—well-organized and extremely safety conscious. Although I was a certified diver, I had never attempted to take photographs during a dive so I was reassured to be in capable hands. I was given a tank, assigned an experienced dive partner and over the side of the boat I went. While I was diving, Deborah did some snorkeling.

The sights below the surface were spectacular—clown fish, parrot fish and turtles moving about amid magnificent formations of coral. There were vibrant tones of color that I had never seen before. I hoped that I would be able to capture a small part of what I was witnessing on film—this was before digital cameras—and struggled with the bulky camera system Henry had lent me.

As I was making adjustments to the camera mechanism, what looked like a large stick drifted towards me from the reef floor. I thought it was a piece of branch coral that had broken loose, and began snapping photos of it. When it approached close enough that I could see it was actually a sea snake, I headed back up to the boat as quickly as I could. Later, when the prints were developed, the "stick" was identified as a highly venomous olive sea snake.

I remained in the boat long enough to recover from my snake fright, and took the plunge again. This next dive lasted until a couple of black tip reef sharks made their appearance in my viewfinder. They were impressive to see, but I didn't wait for them to get too close. Back up to the boat I went, where I was assured that the sharks rarely attacked humans. I wasn't about to test whether they were feeling friendly or were in one of their "rare" moods. Since I'd already taken quite a few photographs, I was content to remain on board until the return to shore.

This was a family vacation, not just a photography excursion for me, and we spent a lot of time experiencing Australia together. We visited an Aboriginal village where Bryan learned to play a digeridoo; he had a knack for music and quickly became adept at the instrument. Jessica and Bryan both loved the dingoes, Australia's ancient dog breed, and tried their best to get us to adopt one as a pet. We brought home a digeridoo, but not a dingo.

Near the end of the trip, we had a scare worse than my shark encounter. Deborah's father Henry suffered a heart attack while we were on a bus ride. Fortunately, the bus happened to be near a hospital when it occurred and Henry was quickly taken into the emergency room. His stay in Australia had to be extended by three weeks until he was well enough to travel back to the States for intricate bypass surgery. Henry recovered, but had to limit his activities thereafter.

That vacation was a special one for our family and remained one of our most cherished experiences, largely because we had been able to enjoy it together. Even if we couldn't all travel together again, we would have the memories of that trip—as well as plenty of photographs to bring those memories into vivid focus.

***

Over the next twenty years, there were many memorable destinations: St. Lucia, where I did some more underwater photography, London, Scotland, Amsterdam, Puerto Rico and the Sea of Cortez. A favorite of the entire family was Hopetown in the Bahamas, where I photographed the venerable candy-striped, kerosene-fueled lighthouse, the last of its kind in the world.

As Bryan and Jessica grew older, they developed interests of their own and spent more time with their friends. Later trips were usually just Deborah and myself, or I would go with a fellow photographer. By 2009, I had already traveled much of the world, but there was one place in particular that I wanted to revisit.

That year, the husband of a long-time patient came to my office for the first time. His name was Mike and he was a photographer, too. He looked over the wildlife photos I had displayed on my walls, some of which were from my *Survivor* experience, and suggested that we go on a photographic outing someday.

I told him, "The only place I really want to visit now is Africa. I loved what little I saw when I was there with *Survivor*, but it wasn't nearly enough." Although the producers had been generous in allowing me to take photos and in arranging outings, the amount of film I was able to bring had been restricted and the opportunities limited.

"Africa sounds good to me," said Mike.

After his dental appointment, Mike went home and returned later that afternoon. He had downloaded a brochure on a photographic safari we might take. While I was with another patient, he showed the brochure to Deborah, who was my office manager again. She looked it over, thought I would enjoy it and told him to book the trip.

So, a few months later, Mike and I were encamped on the Masai Mara national game reserve in Kenya. We were part of a twelve-day photo safari, with about fifty other people, and our tour guide was one of the top wildlife photographers in the world.

This photo safari lived up to all expectations. Not only were there ample opportunities to photograph a wide variety of African wildlife, but there was an open exchange of ideas and technical information on how to improve our results.

Mike and I shared a tent in the camp, and each day everyone with the tour would go out on photo excursions. There were a number of options so that individuals could pursue the subjects that interested them most. Every evening, we would present our best picture of the day to the others for review. By now, the cameras were all digital and there was no delay waiting for film to be developed.

I was especially eager to photograph the region's iconic big game. One of the most difficult photos for me to obtain was of a mother lion and her cub. I was in the back of a Land Rover and it was almost dusk. We knew the lion was somewhere in the grass, but she had settled into a little enclave and wasn't visible. The driver called for me to give up, but I had a feeling that a bit more patience might pay off. "Just a little longer," I said. I opened the door of the vehicle and stretched out on the floor, my camera lens sticking out of the opening. Craning my neck this way and that, I spotted the lions through a gap in the grass—and I got the shot!

Another photo that I presented to the group at our daily session was of a hippopotamus with his mouth gaping open to display enormous, lethal teeth. I noticed during the presentations, though, that the others seemed to get most excited by images of a small, colorful bird called a lilac-breasted roller.

I asked Mike, "What's the big deal about this bird?"

"It's the most beautiful bird in Africa, for one thing," he answered. "And extremely difficult to photograph in flight—moves fast and darts about."

I had noticed that the photographs of the bird were never very sharp. "Well, I can do it," I said, once again speaking before thinking.

He chuckled. "People spend years trying to get a good shot of this bird. And you're going to do it with only three days left in the tour?"

I said that I would. I *had* to now, since I needed to back up my claim.

Sure enough, the lilac-breasted roller got the better of me the first day I tried photographing it in flight. If the composition was good, the image was blurry; if the picture was clear, the bird was darting out of the frame.

I knew it had to be possible to get a quality photo of this bird, and was determined to figure out how. I don't sleep much anyway, so I spent the night studying the matter online and working on the mechanics of my camera. I had a sophisticated DSLR model and had never learned the intricacies of using it in a manual configuration. I had taken some workshops with top instructors, and they always advised, "A camera like that is basically a five-thousand-dollar computer. Run it in automatic and let the camera do the work." Faced with a difficult subject, though, it was clear to me that I had to do the work myself. Left on "auto," my fancy camera wasn't producing good enough results.

In the day or two that remained to us, I got the hang of adjusting the camera's settings manually. By the time we had to pack for home, I had successfully shot photos of the lilac-breasted roller that were judged the best of the group.

This return to Africa remains one of my favorite photo safaris. Not only did I get to spend time with great people in a beautiful land, but it forced me to up my game. I gained a better understanding of the technical aspects of my camera apparatus and developed new skills that I could use in future photography.

***

Probably one of the most unusual inspirations I had for a photo trip came from a movie. I was with several photographer friends, relaxing together after an outdoor photo shoot, and the movie *The Big Year* came on television. The film is about three birders, played by Owen Wilson, Jack Black and Steve Martin, who are competing to spot the most species of birds in one year. During their quest, Owen Wilson's character struggles to find the elusive Snowy Owl.

As we were watching, I mused, "Snowy Owl... that is a really nice looking bird. Let's take a trip and find it. I'd love to get a photo."

My friends laughed. One of them said, "There's a reason the movie is using the Snowy Owl as a tough bird to find. That's because *it's a tough bird to find!*"

Challenge accepted. "We'll find it," I said.

"Where?"

"I'll do some research and let you know."

As a result, in February 2014, I was sitting on frozen Lake Ontario, my entire body numb in minus-thirty-degree weather, waiting for a Snowy Owl to fly into view. I had contacted Christopher Dodds, the top wildlife photographer in Canada and one of the best in the world, and he set up the tour. My friend Randy was the only one of the group that had watched *The Big Year* to accompany me.

We had spent several days hiking through snow, trekking over the frozen lake and camping out on the ice before Dodds located the bird we were seeking. He had spotted a Snowy Owl that was flying back and forth over the lake hunting for voles, a hamster-like rodent that was among the owls' favorite prey.

All we had to do now was set up our tripods on the lake, hope that the owl would come back, hope that it would be in range of our cameras and hope that our fingers wouldn't be too numb to press the button for the shutter. We were in the open, with no windbreaks or shelters.

For three hours, I remained seated in one position. Now and then, I flexed my forefinger to make sure I could move it sufficiently to take a photo if the bird presented itself. Sure enough, the waiting paid off. A beautiful white Snowy Owl soared towards us and I got several photos before it was out of range.

When we returned to the warmth of an Ottawa hotel, Dodds examined the best of my shots and said, "This is great. The only problem is there's a little shadow here on the right eye. You'll want to take that out."

"I don't do any processing," I said. "There's a shadow because of the angle from the sun."

"Oh, you're one of *those*," he groaned. Some photographers want to produce the best-looking print even if it means making some changes afterward—like air-brushing the photo of a model to take out a mole or wrinkle. Others, like me, prefer to keep a photographic image true to the subject.

"Yeah, I think I'll keep it the way it is," I said.

"Photoshop would make it a better print," Dodds suggested again.

I was thrilled to have captured the image of that Snowy Owl and never did do any retouching. For me, part of photography was always about preserving a memory and sharing that moment with others. This trip had been a satisfying enough adventure that I felt no need to change a single thing.

***

Some of the most enjoyable excursions I've experienced have been in recent years. That's because Deborah has usually been able to join me, and I'm always happiest when the two of us are together.

Costa Rica was a place we visited several times. The country is renowned as an ecotourism destination and is home to one of the most beautiful birds in the world: the Resplendent Quetzal. This colorful bird features an iridescent green head, a red body, a yellow beak and a remarkably long, brightly-colored tail. The Resplendent Quetzal is difficult to photograph, largely because its habitat is so remote. The bird is primarily found in the dense cloud forest at an elevation of about two miles.

We did a photo tour in Costa Rica and I was able to get some very nice images of the Resplendent Quetzal. Deborah doesn't do much photography herself, but she got some shots that were better than mine, including some bats during a night shoot and a spectacular photo of a woodpecker.

Deborah and I traveled to a very different climate in 2018. We flew to Norway and took a twelve day cruise on a small ship to the Arctic Circle. The tour was billed as an opportunity to photograph polar bears. There was a lot that we enjoyed about the trip—except that we never even got a glimpse of a polar bear.

We kayaked almost every day. Deborah volunteered to do the paddling so that I would be free to take photos. The kayak was a tandem, and Deborah paddled from the rear seat, steering us through ice floes and around blue glaciers. It was surreal to be immersed in such a unique environment. And, although there were no polar bears, the scenery, the walruses and the puffins proved to be wonderful subjects for my camera lens.

***

One of my favorite countries to visit in the whole world, and one Deborah and I have been to many times, is Italy. Part of the appeal is that these trips provide an opportunity for me to learn more about my heritage. But what I love most about the country is the fact that the people are so genuinely warm and hospitable. Everything is centered around family and food, both of which are important to me.

Although I take a camera or two with me everywhere, I don't come to Italy looking to photograph exotic birds or famous athletes. I try to capture the spirit of the country—the people, the architecture, the landscapes and the food. I've probably photographed every meal I've eaten there!

Two of the cities we most appreciate are Florence and Venice, and both are wonderfully photogenic. The Ponte Vecchio is a centuries-old bridge over the Arno River in Florence and a great subject for photography. The canals of Venice also make for terrific pictures—as well as some romantic gondola rides.

Once, Deborah and I visited Palermo in Sicily. We discovered that our hotel was in a poverty-stricken part of the city, and gangs of young men were hanging out in the streets. I asked the hotel clerk if it was safe for us to walk through the neighborhood.

He pointed to the camera hanging from my neck. "Anybody can see you're a tourist. Of course you're safe."

I didn't understand. "Being a tourist makes me safe?"

"Yes, we need tourists. The Black Hand won't let anything happen to you."

"The 'Black Hand'?" I hadn't heard that term in years, but knew it was a forerunner of the Mafia. "You mean the Mafia?"

He shrugged in the affirmative, but said nothing more aloud.

So, according to him, the Mafia in Palermo kept the neighborhood safe from street crime. It made me feel like I was back in Brooklyn.

The clerk turned out to be correct. Deborah and I had no problems making our way around Palermo. We had a great visit and met some terrific people.

Another place where we met some wonderful people was Positano. This is a picturesque cliffside village on the Amalfi Coast, south of Naples where my grandfather had been born. Deborah and I became such good friends with the owners of a restaurant in Positano that we invited them to our home for Thanksgiving. They flew to the United States and we were able to share our culture and hospitality with them as they had so generously done with us.

To me, that's what travel is all about. The sights and the photographs are nice, but connecting with other people is the real joy.

15. At the Microphone

With my penchant for talking and my love of sports, I suppose I'm a natural candidate to host a sports talk show. I had never imagined doing such a job, but I was presented with the opportunity and decided to give it a try.

It turned out that the talent agent I had met at the Crystal Reel Awards was not making idle party talk when she'd said that she wanted to represent me. A week after the awards ceremony, she telephoned and asked, "How would you like to be the host of your own TV talk show?"

I had been trained in dentistry, not journalism, and wasn't sure what hosting a program would involve. "What would I do?" I asked.

"You would talk."

I could do that. "What kind of a show?"

She told me that the name of the show was *Sports Hotline*. It would be produced by the PBS affiliate in Daytona Beach, and was scheduled to air on Tuesday nights.

My own sports talk show? I thought. I was in!

The next Friday, I went to the WCEU studio at Daytona Beach Community College for an audition. The producer of *Sports Hotline* was Bruce E. Dunn, a highly regarded television professional who had worked for ABC Sports and won several Emmy awards. Bruce had planned a thirteen-part series, outlined the topics and already arranged for many of the guests.

My audition consisted of hosting a complete half-hour mock episode. Bruce explained that he had to see how I performed in a full show and how I handled the unexpected. In public broadcasting, there were no commercials they could cut to—I would have to keep going for the duration and maintain viewers' interest. To see if I could deal with the unknown, he wouldn't even tell me what sport we'd be discussing during the audition episode.

At first, I was instructed to read prepared lines from a teleprompter. I stumbled over them; I'm simply not good at saying someone else's words. Bruce then let me loose to speak for myself and it went much better.

The guest for the show was Scott Hoch, who had just won his eleventh PGA tournament. It was then that I discovered I would have to spend thirty minutes discussing golf, a sport about which I knew absolutely nothing. Hoch walked onto the set and I introduced him to the audience. I began with a confession: I held my right thumb and forefinger about an eighth of an inch apart and said, "This is how much I know about golf."

So I winged it, following up with natural questions and comments to whatever Hoch said, and we had a smoothly flowing conversation. Then a voice in my ear announced, "Doc, we have caller." That must have been one of the surprises the producers had planned for me.

I momentarily looked around at the ceiling, silently wondering, *Where? What caller?* Quickly recovering my wits, I said, "Go ahead caller."

It was either a crank or a miniature golf aficionado. "I'm having trouble with my stroke," the caller said. "I can get the ball into the dragon's mouth, but it doesn't come out its butt like it's supposed to. Can you give me some advice?"

"Certainly," I said. "You need to dial the correct number: 1-800-*Fuggedaboutit*."

The entire crew cracked up laughing. I passed the audition.

***

Sports Hotline debuted in April, 2003. A major reason I was attracted to doing the program was Bruce Dunn's vision for the show. Each week, the focus would be on a different sport, and would cover high school, college and professional levels, as well as both men's and women's leagues. Guests would include players, coaches, officials and trainers. Not only would the programs be inclusive and diverse, but they would promote the positive aspects of sport and highlight the dedication and hard work of the athletes.

When it came to being positive, basketball player Darrell Armstrong proved to be one of the most inspiring examples of that quality. I knew Darrell well; he had been playing for the Orlando Magic since 1995 and the two of us had become friends. He graciously agreed to be part of *Sports Hotline*'s basketball episode.

Darrell's ambition since an early age was to be an NBA basketball player. He was a good athlete in high school and college, but stood barely six feet tall and was not selected in the league's draft. Undeterred, Darrell continued playing in lower-level and international leagues. He was named Player of the Year in Cyprus, and then moved on to Spain where he was finally noticed by the NBA and signed by the Orlando Magic.

With the Magic, Darrell epitomized the team's "Heart and Hustle" slogan, always working hard and giving his very best effort. Although not a starter, his contributions coming in off the bench helped lead the team to seven post-season appearances. In 1999, he won the NBA's Sixth Man of the Year Award. His work ethic and positive attitude made him a favorite with the fans.

In discussing his difficult path to the NBA, Darrell said, "It's all about determination, passion and hard work."

I commented, "If you believe in your dreams, you can make them come true."

"That's exactly right, Doc. And the kids out there need to know that."

Darrell was not only inspirational in his playing, but off the court as well. He had been born premature, suffered some health problems as a child and wanted to help those in a similar situation. He partnered with Florida Hospital and launched the Darrell Armstrong Foundation for Premature Babies, which has now been helping children for more than twenty years.

***

Although I was a fan of sports in general, my first love was baseball and I was especially pleased with the lineup of guests we had scheduled for the baseball show. Among them were a Little League World Series champion, a retired major league umpire, and a women's softball player.

The umpire was Harry Wendelstedt, who lived nearby and came into the studio for an interview. He had umpired in the National League for thirty-three years, working more than four thousand games and five World Series. Wendelstedt also ran professional baseball's foremost school for training umpires.

Wendelstedt had a deep love of the game and expressed concern about the diminishing number of younger fans. "Kids don't want to watch a three-hour game that ends up with a one-nothing score," he observed. "They want more scoring and a faster pace."

I agreed with him. I had always loved baseball, but my son Bryan had no interest in the game. Like many kids of his generation, he found video games and technology to be more enticing than a leisurely ballgame.

I asked Wendelstedt what changes he would make to the game. His main suggestion was a pitch clock: If pitchers were limited in the amount of time they had between each pitch, it would shorten the games and increase the action.

We also discussed his training school and what life was like for an umpire. I knew baseball from the viewpoint of a fan and an amateur player, and was fascinated to hear the perspective of a veteran umpire. I think my interview with Wendelstedt provided the audience with some important insights into the game.

Coincidentally, a few years after Harry Wendelstedt was on the show, one of his former students became a patient of mine. Troy Soos graduated in the same class as major league umpires John Hirschbeck and Gerry Davis. Although Troy didn't continue his umpiring career, he went on to write the Mickey Rawlings baseball mysteries. He liked my sports photographs, I liked his books, we both loved baseball and we soon became good friends. When Troy wrote his novel about the New York Yankees, *The Tomb That Ruth Built*, he named one of the pitchers "Carl Bilancione." So now I can tell people that I pitched for the Yankees!

We also had a real pitcher—one of the best—on *Sports Hotline*. Frank Viola, known as "Sweet Music," was a three-time All-Star who won a Cy Young Award with the Minnesota Twins and was named Most Valuable Player in the 1987 World Series. The two of us had hit it off the first time we met years earlier; we were both Italian guys from New York who loved food and baseball.

Frank was happy to be a guest on the show, but he was coaching his son's high school baseball team at the time and couldn't come into the studio. So we went to McCracken Field near the Citrus Bowl in Orlando and taped an interview with him before the team's practice.

One of the things I asked him was, "Having won both a Cy Young Award and a World Series MVP, which of those was your favorite?"

"Winning the World Series," he answered without hesitation. "The Cy Young was great, but the World Series is really a team effort. Winning it is what every ballclub works for all year long."

The answer didn't surprise me. Frank Viola was a thoughtful man who was all about teamwork and sportsmanship. He emphasized those qualities to the boys he coached and inspired them to pursue their dreams.

***

A couple of other old friends participated in different shows to discuss their sports. One was Greg Sacks, who did the stunt driving for Tom Cruise in *Days of Thunder* and had gotten me onto the movie set. He joined me in the studio for an episode on racing.

Greg was very humble man and another example of how hard work and dedication could pay off. He had grown up on Long Island, not far from a racetrack, and always loved cars and racing. But auto racing was a very expensive sport and a tough one to break into unless you had the money for your own car and equipment. Greg's family was of modest means, so he had to work his way up, taking any opportunity he could get to gain driving experience. He worked primarily as a research-and-development driver.

The highlight of his career was winning the Firecracker 400 at Daytona in 1985. He had some subsequent struggles, including a life-threatening crash while driving for Cale Yarborough, but he remained committed to the sport and persevered, never losing his passion and optimism.

Another guest whom I'd known for years was Ethan Zohn, winner of *Survivor Africa*. Not only had Ethan and I been together in Africa, but we were both affiliated with Fairleigh Dickinson University; I was an alumnus and Ethan had coached both men's and women's soccer at the school. In addition to coaching the FDU team, Ethan had been a professional soccer player himself for several years. He phoned in during our soccer episode.

Ethan was another *Survivor* cast member who was heavily involved in charitable work. He helped organize a charity called Grassroots Soccer, using some of his *Survivor* winnings to finance the fledgling organization. As Ethan explained on the program, Grassroots Soccer was formed to address the HIV/AIDS crisis in Africa. It uses soccer to educate and inspire young people, while providing them with information on HIV prevention.

During its season of thirteen episodes, *Sports Hotline* was able to feature something for every sports fan. We did shows devoted to fishing, hockey, track and field, swimming and diving, figure skating, skateboarding and the Olympics. We provided a spotlight for athletes and a forum for discussion. When the series concluded, Bruce Dunn and I agreed that it had been every bit as successful as he had envisioned and I was proud to have been a part of it.

The station executives seemed to feel the same way. A different program had been slated to take our time slot when our run was over, but after one episode it was dropped. I got a phone call the next day asking if I was available to come back. Bruce and I quickly sketched out a new series of programs, and *Sports Hotline* returned to television the following week for one more season.

***

About six years after *Sports Hotline*'s final episode, I became cohost of a radio show. This venture came about as the result of another "put up or shut up" situation. The latter wasn't a possibility for me, so I had to do the former.

I was at the Orlando Arena with my friend Tony "Ace" Rossi, watching the Magic game and listening to a play-by-play on the radio. "Those announcers are terrible,"

I said. "No personalities at all—they sound like they're announcing a funeral."

"You think you could do better?" Ace asked.

"In a New York minute." Clearly, I hadn't learned my lesson. That was the same answer I had given my office manager Dawn when she'd asked if I could handle being on *Survivor*—and that had led to me starving in a boma in Africa.

"You don't know anything about statistics," Ace pointed out.

"Who cares? Does anybody really need to hear 'That was the seventeenth ground-rule double hit by a left-handed first baseman from Iowa since the advent of interleague play'? A good announcer just has to say what happens and be enthusiastic about the game. It's about *entertainment*."

The next day I got a call from Ace. "We have a meeting with Cox Radio in Orlando. They have an open slot for a radio show. So put your money where your mouth is."

My affiliation with the Magic had helped Ace convince the program manager to meet with us. We went to the station, and the first thing we were asked was, "What do you know about radio?"

Ace and I answered in near unison, "Nothing."

"Well, what do you know about talk shows?"

I said, "I used to have my own sports talk show on television," and told him about *Sports Hotline*.

The manager acknowledged that my TV experience would help, but he remained skeptical about giving a time slot to two guys who simply walked in off the street and said they wanted to have a radio show. "Television is different," he told us. "You have visuals, so you don't need to be talking all the time. With radio, you can't have any dead air."

I assured him, "The way Ace and I talk, there won't be a second of silence. I guarantee you that."

That's how a couple of big-mouthed sports fans went on the air with a weekly program called "Ace and the Doc." And we immediately became a hit!

***

Ace and I made no pretense of being journalists. We were simply fans who loved sports and could express our enthusiasm verbally. Just as with *Sports Hotline*, our goal was to highlight the positive qualities of the players and the teams. We didn't overanalyze games, never harangued a player about a poor performance and were never out to embarrass anyone or put them on the spot. As a result of our positive approach, we found it easy to get athletes and other sports figures as guests for the show.

We even landed one guest whom legitimate sports journalists had been trying to book for years without success. Leigh Steinberg was the premier sports agent for professional football players, famous as the inspiration for the movie *Jerry Maguire*. He represented a record number of NFL first round draft picks and permanently changed the financial dynamics between players and owners.

Steinberg had a firm policy against doing interviews, but Ace had a friend who was able to arrange one with us. By this time, *Ace and the Doc* had moved to the ESPN station in Orlando and our listening audience had grown.

The agent discussed the need for professional football players to receive the large salaries he negotiated for them. He pointed out that they have a playing lifespan of only a few years, suffer physical damage that sometimes lasts for the rest of their lives, and that they need to make sure their families are financially secure for years to come. Steinberg said, "The owners hate me and I don't care. I don't care about them and I don't really care about football. My concern is the players I represent and making sure that they get what they and their families deserve."

Steinberg had agreed to give us a ten-minute telephone interview, but stayed on for almost an hour. He provided a perspective many of us had never considered, and it made for a riveting program.

***

One of the wildest radio shows we did was a live broadcast that I hosted from Rome. *Ace and the Doc* was a live, one-hour show that aired at the same time every Thursday night. I was going to have to miss being in the studio one of those evenings, though, because I had a vacation to Italy planned. Instead of leaving it to Ace to go solo, I decided to see if it was feasible for me to call in. And if I was going to call in, I thought it should be from a sports venue.

I did some research and found that there was a sports bar in Rome that was run by a Pittsburgh Steelers fan. This was perfect! Ace was from Pittsburgh and one of my friends joining me on the trip was Rick Susi, who loved all the Pittsburgh sports teams. I contacted the owner of the bar and he agreed to let me do a broadcast and interview his customers.

Although La Botticella Birreria was only blocks from the Vatican and the Coliseum, it looked like it could have been a neighbor of Three Rivers Stadium. When we arrived at the bar with our equipment, the first thing I saw was a Steelers sticker on the front door. Prominently displayed inside was a large white banner that read "You're in Steelers Country." The walls were festooned with Pittsburgh jerseys, autographed photos of the players and other memorabilia.

Because of the time difference, it was well after midnight in Rome when we did the live remote. The bar was packed anyway, with fans and patrons enthusiastic about taking part in the broadcast.

My first interview was with the owner. I was curious to find out how he had come to open a Pittsburgh Steelers bar in downtown Rome. He explained that he had lived in Canada as a boy during the 1970s, when Pittsburgh dominated football with its "Steel Curtain" dynasty. The man fell in love with the sport, the team and the players—Terry Bradshaw, Lynn Swann, Franco Harris, "Mean Joe" Greene, John Stallworth and Jack Lambert, among others. When he moved back to Rome, he decided to share his passion by opening the sports bar.

I also spoke with a number of the bar's patrons, who enjoyed the camaraderie and excitement that La Botticella Birreria provided them. Love of sport can certainly transcend national boundaries and customs!

***

Ace and I were on the air from 2010 to 2011, but we didn't remain with the same station. Radio was changing and there were frequent mergers and purchases that caused us to move. No matter the call letters of our station, we had large audiences and expanded the program from one hour to two to satisfy our listeners' demand.

The end came because we were too successful. Ace and I went into the radio station one day to find the set and equipment being dismantled. Without consulting us, the station had sold our program to another outlet which wanted us to do the show on a daily basis instead of weekly. That would have been great news if Ace and I were in the broadcasting business, but we weren't. We never received a dime in payment for what we did; we were just a couple of fans sharing our love of sports with the listeners. I had a full-time dental practice and Ace had a job in marketing. Neither of us could give up our careers for the radio show, but it was a fun run while it lasted.

On both television and radio, I loved talking sports and I'm grateful to have had the chance to share my passion with an audience. And, although I no longer have a microphone, I still talk.

16. An Unlucky Break

Despite my love of rich Italian food, I had made into my fifties in overall good health. I was always active—playing sports, running marathons, diving and bicycling. One of the bike rides I did each year was the "MS 150 Breakaway Ride" organized by the Florida chapter of the Multiple Sclerosis Society. The route was from Miami to Key Largo and back, totaling 150 miles over two days. A very good friend of mine had been afflicted with the disease for years, and I wanted to show support and help raise awareness.

A few days after Christmas in 2014, Deborah and I had plans to visit some friends at lunchtime and do a little cooking together. We were going to prepare Italian dishes for them, and they were going to teach us some Russian recipes. That morning, a couple of hours before we needed to leave, I decided to get in a quick twenty-mile ride to help prepare for the upcoming MS 150.

I am always very safety conscious. Before leaving the house, I checked the pressure of the tires on my light Cervelo racing bike. Then I donned a Kevlar helmet, knee pads and padded gloves. I placed my cell phone in its mount on the handle bar in case I needed to make an emergency call.

With everything in order, I set out down our driveway for a nice Sunday ride through Winter Springs and Oviedo. And then—

***

What exactly followed "and then" remains a blank to me. My brain is missing that memory.

When I regained consciousness, I was sprawled on the asphalt of the bike trail, my Cervelo lying nearby. The frame of the bicycle was broken. Although I didn't know it yet, I had suffered a bad break too.

There was no collision with a car or a tree. I could only piece together what had probably happened months later: While coming down an incline at a high speed, the front tire had blown, the bike frame slammed down, and I flew headfirst over the handlebar.

My first actual recollection, although fuzzy, was of a woman passerby asking me, "Are you alright?"

"Just fine," I answered automatically, having no idea what shape I was really in.

I remained on the ground for a while, trying to gather my wits and figure out what had happened. In addition to seeing the remnants of my bike, I noticed a lot of blood. It dripped down from my face and glued my shirt to my chest and shoulder.

My cell phone was still on the handlebar. I crawled over to it and called Deborah. "Bryan needs to come pick me up," I said.

"Why? What happened?"

"I've had an accident. Pretty bad, and my bike is broken."

Deborah offered to get me herself, but I told her, "No, I'm a mess and I don't want you to see me like this. Send Bryan. Tell him to take my Jeep." I gave her my location and waited.

When I saw Bryan drive up, I picked up the bicycle—I don't know how—and carried it to the car. As my son opened the back of the Jeep to put it in, I said, "Take me home. I need a bath and I have to get cleaned up." Some blood was drying on my shirt, but fresh blood continued to trickle down my face. My helmet was still on my head, and it was covering up additional damage.

Bryan helped me into the passenger's seat and quickly looked me over. Instead of taking me home, he drove directly to the nearest emergency room. In this case, his medical acumen was sounder than mine.

I was taken into the emergency room, and again my memory isn't clear—between shock, morphine and trauma, my mind was pretty muddled. I distinctly recall the doctor asking Bryan if I'd been wearing a helmet. Bryan answered that I had, but that it had broken in the accident. He went to the car and brought it in to show the doctor.

The helmet was fractured at the left temple. "This is *Kevlar*," the doctor observed, as he turned it over in his hands. "Do you realize how powerful the impact must have been to crack this helmet? Kevlar can stop a *bullet*!"

"I know," replied Bryan quietly. Having served in the Army's 82nd Airborne, he was familiar with the material.

"Well, it saved your father's life," the doctor said.

A radiologist ran three CT scans on me. It was determined that I had fractured my T8 vertebrae in four places and just missed severing my spinal column. There were also numerous contusions and lacerations to much of my face and upper body, but these were far less serious.

By now, Deborah had arrived. I heard the doctor tell her and Bryan, "With an injury like this, he could be paralyzed. We need to transport him to a facility with a trauma unit." I wish I'd been unconscious when he said the word "paralyzed" because hearing that certainly didn't make me feel any better.

I was transported by ambulance to a larger medical center. It happened to be the same one where my daughter Jessica was working as a cardiac nurse. I wished more than once that I could have been under her care, because I know it would have been better than what I actually received.

After waiting twelve hours in the ER, I was assigned to a room where I then had to await evaluation from a neurosurgeon. Twenty-four hours later, I was informed that no one could find the neurosurgeon. I was getting pretty frustrated with the way things were going.

Two days after I had been admitted, no one had even cleaned the blood and dirt from my face, so Deborah carefully did that herself. She stayed with me every minute that I was in the hospital.

When the neurosurgeon finally showed up, he simply announced, "You'll be fitted for a body brace. Wear it for six months, and if that doesn't work I'll do surgery." Before I could ask a question, he ducked back out of the room.

On the morning of New Year's Eve, three days after the accident, I checked myself out of the hospital and Deborah took me home. I was wearing a body brace called a "turtle shell" that enclosed me from waist to neck. As soon as we got to the house, I made an appointment to see a different neurosurgeon.

***

Although I was still in a lot of pain, being home was much more comfortable than that hospital. The care I received from my family and friends was exceptional. In my condition, I needed help with basic life activities and they were always there to provide it.

My mobility was severely limited. The turtle shell that encased my torso was necessarily restrictive. Along with the rigid material of the shell, there was a bar that pressed on my sternum to keep me from moving too much. I was also physically unable to raise my arms above shoulder height. Finally, I was not allowed to lie on my back; I would have to sleep sitting upright. In order for me to sleep as comfortably as possible, some friends modified a plush recliner so that I couldn't extend it into the reclining position. The brace could be removed for showers, but I needed assistance washing. Thanks to everyone's help, all my needs were taken care of. I couldn't have been in better hands.

To determine my long-term course of treatment, Deborah took me to one of the top neurosurgeons in the area. He suggested surgery, specifically a procedure called a kyphoplasty. As he described it, "I'll fill the breaks in your vertebrae with bone cement, and a few days after the procedure you can go back to work pain-free."

"There's no such thing as 'bone cement,'" I pointed out to him. "Tell me what the actual material is."

He was taken aback by my response. "Why? What do you do for a living?"

"I'm a dentist."

He gave me the chemical name of the material he was proposing to inject into my back.

"That's *glue*," I said. "Won't that degrade over time, and chip off?"

"Well, yes," he admitted. "Then we go back in and clean out the chips."

As a dentist, I had always advised the course of treatment to my patients that I would want for my own teeth. The neurosurgeon and I were about the same age and build. I asked him, "If you were me, would you have the kyphoplasty?"

He stared up at the ceiling and rubbed his chin. "Well, I would have to think about it." I could tell by the fact that he didn't look at me when replying that the true answer was probably "no."

"I'll think about it, too," I said.

He tried to press me. "We can schedule you for Friday."

"If I stay in the body cast instead, will my back heal on its own?"

"Possibly," he answered. "The breaks in the vertebrae will fill in with fibrous tissue. You'll probably have some ongoing discomfort, though, and eventually you'll lose about an inch of height."

Deborah took me home and I carefully considered the options. I contacted the neurosurgeon and told him I would stick with the body brace and see if it healed sufficiently on its own. If not, I would go ahead with the surgery.

I then began six months of life as a debilitated turtle.

***

Although I was financially secure enough to stay home under the care of my family, I had other people's livelihoods to consider. I was the sole practitioner in a one-man dental office, supported by a staff of assistants, hygienists and a receptionist. Without me, there wasn't much for them to do.

My accountant advised me to shut down the practice and lay off the employees until I could return to work. I told him I couldn't do that to my staff; they had been loyal to me, and I would be loyal to them. I had decided to continue paying their full salaries, and I instructed him to make withdrawals from my retirement account if necessary.

That took care of my staff, but I also had long-time patients who depended on me for regular treatment. I made some inquiries and found a very proficient dentist who was able to come in two days a week to cover for me during the first part of the year.

By June, I was able to remove the brace and return to my practice, working limited hours. No matter how short my work day, though, I was in pain every evening. I realized that I would not be able to continue. As difficult as it was for me to accept, I knew that I would have to give up the practice that I had spent thirty years building.

At the end of the year, after making sure that all my employees were lined up with new jobs, I sold the practice and the office suite. I agreed to continue working on a part-time basis for the new owner so that I could still treat the patients who had put their trust in me for so many years.

***

My life after the accident was very different from what it had been before. Ever since I was a boy, I had dreamed of being a dentist. Now, after having spent three decades building my own practice, it was no longer mine. The activities I had so enjoyed—running, biking, diving—were over with, too. Still, I knew that, overall, I was a very lucky man with a great life and I adapted as best I could to the new reality.

I still kept my hand in dentistry, treating patients a couple of days a week and mentoring other dentists. In order to stay in physical shape, I found new ways of exercising. I never rode a real bicycle again, but I joined the local YMCA and worked out on a stationary spinning bike—which led to a lot of jokes from my family that I should probably still wear a helmet.

As the neurosurgeon had predicted, I lost some height, but being five-ten instead of five-eleven is really no hardship. Other than that, the only trouble I still have is a little backache at the end of the day, and I can handle that.

I accepted the limitations of my new life, truly grateful that the long-term effects of the accident hadn't been worse. Unfortunately, as I continued my recovery, a couple of people close to me were soon facing health scares of their own.

17. Revelations

In early 2016, my father began mentioning that he was thinking of moving out of New Jersey. He was eighty years old, no longer working, and claimed that he was in the mood for a different environment. That seemed odd to me. My father had always been a city guy. He liked to hang out with his friends in their social clubs and gamble in Atlantic City.

Within a few months, he started to hint that the destination he had in mind was Florida. The weather was warmer, he said, and my mother would enjoy living closer to Jessica and Bryan. This, too, seemed out of character. My father had never given my mother's feelings or wishes any consideration.

During the summer, he announced his plan: He and my mother would move to Florida and find a place close to Deborah and me. We were happy at the news; we all enjoyed my mother's company and had learned to tolerate my father's.

By now, we owned a condo at Daytona Beach Shores that we used as a weekend getaway. Deborah and I discussed it, and invited them to live at the condo as long as they wanted, rent-free. My father jumped at the offer.

In September, I flew to New Jersey. My parents had sold their townhouse and were ready for the big move to the Sunshine State. Despite the limitations from my back injury, I helped them pack their belongings into a U-Haul and drove it down to Daytona.

They moved into our condo, a beautiful three-bedroom unit on the tenth floor with a balcony and a spectacular view of the ocean. My mother was thrilled with the spacious accommodations and my father didn't voice any complaints, which is about as enthusiastic as he gets. Everything seemed to be going smoothly. But I knew there was something unsaid behind the move and I wanted to find out what it was.

I learned the truth from my cousin Leo. My father had told him that he thought he was dying. Since he knew that Deborah and I were the only ones in our family who would care for my mother if he was gone, he decided to move closer to us.

My father could have been straightforward with us about his reason for moving to Florida. Deborah and I would have been more than willing to take care of my mother under any circumstances. There was no need for subterfuge. But doing things honestly was never my father's style.

***

My parents settled into the beach condo and seemed to be enjoying their new home. We were very happy to have them near us, and began spending time with them, especially with my mother. We took her out for Chinese food, which she loved, and Deborah gave her manicures and treated her to shopping trips. I didn't reveal to my father what I had learned from cousin Leo; I would let him tell me in his own time.

One day, my father was sitting alone on the balcony, contentedly working on his third or fourth beer. When I brought him another, he started to get in a chatty mood and I sat down next to him. I thought it would be nice to shoot the breeze with him, father and son.

I asked him something I'd wondered about for years. "Hey Dad, how did you get the name 'Rocky'?" Everyone assumed it was because his hands were rock-hard from working on the docks, but I knew that he'd had the nickname before he became a longshoreman.

"Well, that's kind of a funny story," he said with a chuckle. "When I was stationed in Newfoundland—I must have been seventeen then—I was in the PX. That's where your mother worked and so did your Aunt Ruby. I was in the checkout line, and the guy ahead of me was hassling Ruby. He said he wouldn't pay his bill unless she gave him a kiss. You know how your mother and her sisters are—*very* religious and *very* strict. A kiss was never going to happen, but the guy kept pressing her. I finally said to him, 'Just pay the lady what you owe and leave her alone.' He didn't like me butting in. The guy turned around and pulled back his arm to throw a punch. So I popped him one right on the jaw. Knocked him out cold." My father laughed at the memory and took another sip of beer.

"So that's how you got the name 'Rocky'?"

"Oh, there's more. It turned out the guy was an officer—a lieutenant, I think. And officers don't like being hit by enlisted men. I was summoned to the base captain, who was steaming. He said to me, 'So you're the little Guinea from New York who thinks he's a tough guy.' I tried to explain why I'd hit the lieutenant, but the captain didn't care. 'Let's see how tough you are,' he said. 'You're going into the ring with the base boxing champion tomorrow. We'll see how you do against *him*.' I told the captain I didn't want to box, but he didn't want to hear it.

"The next day I showed up at the base gym. There was a pretty good crowd gathered around for the show—they were all sure I was going to get the crap beat out of me. The manager of the gym laced the gloves on me and he was grinning. For some reason, he was especially eager to see me take a beating. Well, the bell rang and we came out of our corners. I threw one punch and that was all it took for me to knock out the base boxing champ! He was out *cold*.

"The manager was furious. He screamed at me, 'Who the hell do you think you are, you little Guinea? Rocky Marciano?' After that, everybody started calling me 'Rocky.' And they stopped calling me 'little Guinea.' Then they wanted me to join the boxing team and I refused. So I lost a stripe—got busted down to seaman second class. I didn't care about the loss of rank. Your mother's family thought I was some kind of hero for handling the guy who was bothering Ruby."

I laughed. I thought it was a great story and was happy to be having an enjoyable father-son chat. We didn't have many of those.

My father went on, "Your mother wasn't the first woman I wanted to marry, you know."

I hadn't known that, and was totally surprised to hear it. "She wasn't?"

My father shook his empty beer bottle, indicating that I needed to get him another. When I did, he opened it and proceeded to explain, "When I first joined the Navy, they stationed me at Guantanamo. And I met a Cuban girl—beautiful, long dark hair, big bright eyes, great body. Her family owned a nightclub not far from the base. This was before Castro, and there was a lot of fun to be had in Cuba in those days. This particular club was off limits to U. S. military, but I'd dress in civvies, she'd get me in and we'd have some wild times. I was madly in love with this girl and I asked her to marry me. She said 'yes' and her family was all for it, but I was underage. I was only sixteen when I joined the Navy."

I knew that his early enlistment was to avoid jail time and that my grandfather had to appear in court to sign his papers for him. "What happened?" I prodded.

"I needed my dad's permission, so I wrote to him. He wrote me back and said there was no way I was marrying some foreigner, especially no Hispanic. I got his letter ten days before we were to ship out, so I hid out on the boat that whole time."

"You didn't tell the girl?"

"Nah, what would be the point? The marriage wasn't going to happen, and that was that. Why should I have had to deal with listening to her cry about it?" He laughed. "She and her family were running around all over trying to find out what happened to me. I suppose they finally caught on when the ship pulled out."

My father actually seemed amused at having left the girl and her family in the lurch. He was brave enough to punch out a Navy officer, but lacked the courage to face a woman he claimed to have loved. I was sorry to learn that about him.

Pausing only for another swallow of beer, he added, "Almost the same thing happened when I wanted to marry your mother."

I wasn't sure that I wanted to hear about it, but was curious.

"I was seventeen then, so I still needed my father's permission. I wrote to him and told him about your mother. I thought her being Canadian was close enough to being an American, but he refused. He said there's no way he'd let me marry a foreigner. This time, I figured out how to deal with him. I wrote another letter, saying if he wouldn't let me marry her then he needed to send me ten grand because she was pregnant."

"*What?*"

My father laughed. "She wasn't, of course, but my father didn't know that. He wasn't about to give me any money, so he signed the papers for us to marry."

I suddenly knew why my grandparents had spat at my mother when they first met her and called her a whore. "You never told them the truth, did you?" I said.

"Nah, why should I?"

"Because they treated Mom *horribly*. Your lie caused her a lot of pain!"

He shrugged. I think he was proud of pulling one over on his father and didn't really care about the long-term harm he'd done. While we lived with my grandparents in Brooklyn, both my mother and I were scorned and treated as outcasts. I realized now, that in their eyes, my mother was a "whore" and I was her "bastard."

I leaned back in my chair and stared out at the horizon, dumbfounded. So much for a friendly father-son chat.

Still talkative, he began telling me about the mistress he'd had for decades and what fun she was. I got up and went back inside. I didn't want to hear any more of his stories.

***

My parent only lived in our condo for a few months. My father was soon bored by the beach and lamented the lack of "action." He wanted a house, so Deborah and I helped them purchase a home of their own not far from Orlando. They moved in shortly before Christmas. When my mother wanted to put up decorations for the holiday, my father refused and Deborah and I did that for them, too.

In January, my mother developed a cold that wouldn't go away. Since I knew a lot of the top physicians in Florida, I arranged for her to see a pulmonologist. The exam revealed a spot on her lung as well as a lump in her breast.

My father had accompanied her to the appointment and was coughing as usual. He'd been a heavy smoker for seventy years and had a cough as far back as I can remember. By now, he often sounded like a diesel truck with a misfiring engine. The doctor asked him if he was okay, and my father said that he'd been to the emergency room the day before because he'd been coughing up blood. The doctor immediately ran tests on him, too. The diagnosis was stage 3 lung cancer. My father still had said nothing to us about the fact that he thought he was dying. Now, it appeared that his prediction might prove to be accurate.

Fortunately, my mother recovered quickly after a lumpectomy and was cancer-free. My father's case was more difficult. I arranged for his treatment with the top oncologist in Florida. Because of the location of the mass, surgery wasn't an option. A regimen of chemotherapy, radiation and drugs was the only course of action and it lasted for months. Throughout that time, I was continuing my dental practice part-time, taking my parents to doctors, scheduling their appointments and driving back-and-forth to their house to make sure they had food and all the other necessities.

By the summer, my father had completed his treatment and recovered. He was no longer dying, and he began making plans for his next move.

***

My father started to get grouchier and his temper flared unpredictably. He began lashing out at my mother, subjecting her to vicious tirades. As often as Deborah or I could, we would pick up my mother and bring her to our home where she could be safe among loved ones. But that was only when my father permitted her to go.

My mother had always been submissive to my father. She did nothing without his approval, voiced no opinions unless they were in keeping with his own and meekly accepted whatever abuse he inflicted on her. Partly it was because she was very old-fashioned and took the "obey" part of her marriage vows literally. Also, I believe she'd become something of an emotional hostage to him over the years and she'd come to accept her role as captive.

Things became so bad that I had to call the police to do a wellness check. To my father, calling the police was like collaborating with the enemy and a complete betrayal. As a result, I was banished from their home.

Finally, my father had a particularly explosive tantrum and announced to my mother that he was sick of her and leaving her forever. He got into his car and drove to New Jersey. The car was already packed, so he must have planned his departure before the tantrum. My poor mother cried uncontrollably and kept asking over and over, "What did I do wrong?"

In New Jersey, my father put a deposit on a new house near Toms River. It was only a few miles from where his mistress lived. She was the reason he wanted to leave Florida.

A few weeks later, he drove back down. He stayed long enough to sell the house in Florida and reconcile with my distraught mother. Then they moved away from us, to the new home in New Jersey. My father now had things exactly as he wanted them and as they had been for almost half a century: My mother took care of the house and cooked his meals, and he had a "goomah" nearby for his pleasure.

***

I wish I could speak better of my father. I'm sure every son would like to think that his dad is a great guy. But too often, for too many of us, that's simply not the case. And I have to be truthful.

Years ago, not long after I returned from *Survivor* and my father was home from his stay in New Jersey State Prison, I was visiting my parents at their townhome. I remembered the inmates at Lewisburg Penitentiary telling me of the violence that went on behind prison walls, and I asked my father how his experience had been.

"No problems," he said. "Easy living and three meals a day."

"But everybody hears about those awful things that happen to guys in prison," Even Dr. DeVos, the Lewisburg dentist, had his throat cut, I recalled. "Nobody gave you any trouble?"

My father smiled. "Nobody touched me."

Of course, I realized. With his affiliation, no one would dare.

"That whole thing was a setup anyway," my father said. "I should've never been in there. The cops wanted me to name names, I wouldn't, and so they made me the fall guy. If they knew anything about me, they should have known I would never talk." He paused and added emphatically, "I am no rat."

To my father, and men like him, violence, deceit, infidelity, theft and intimidation were all perfectly acceptable. As long as you weren't a rat, you were an okay guy. So, although I can't say much else that's positive, I will give my father credit for the one virtue that he considered most important: He was no rat.

18. A Real Survivor

We always knew it was a possibility, but that didn't lessen the impact when my beautiful wife of almost forty years got the diagnosis. Breast cancer, the same disease that had taken the lives of her mother and grandmother, was now attacking Deborah.

Because of her family history, Deborah had always been conscientious about her checkups. Even if the disease did strike her, regular exams should catch it early and improve her chances of dealing with it successfully. It was a sound strategy, but sometimes cancer can hit fast and spread quickly.

A few days before Christmas in 2019, Deborah went for her regularly scheduled exam. Not one, but *three* lumps were discovered. We were told that she needed an ultrasound and a biopsy immediately. There weren't a lot of medical people working during the holidays, so "immediately" was a difficult time frame to schedule. I phoned everyone I knew who might be able to help, and finally was able to get appointments for her. I also had to find a good oncologist and have Deborah's records and test results transferred—another challenge at that time of year.

On January 6, I took her to the oncologist, who was a top-rated physician and one of the leading specialists in her field. She had reviewed all of the files, examined Deborah and confirmed the dreaded diagnosis: Deborah had breast cancer and it was in an advanced stage.

***

Deborah required surgery as soon as possible. However, assembling the necessary medical team to do the work takes some time. I first contacted someone I knew at Sloan-Kettering in New York, the top cancer treatment center in the country. The earliest they could schedule surgery wouldn't be until April, three months away. Meanwhile, every day we were getting more worried. To go from a clean bill of health at her previous checkup to three lumps having been found during her most recent exam meant that the cancer was probably aggressive and could be spreading quickly. It had to be removed before it metastasized.

Fortunately, an excellent team was available at Florida Hospital in Orlando, including an oncologic surgeon and a plastic surgeon. On January 24, Deborah underwent a double mastectomy. She was on the operating table for ten hours.

The surgery went well, and the doctors believed they had removed all of the cancerous tissue. But that was only the first step in her treatment.

**

Deborah's battle to recover lasted the entire year of 2020. I immediately took an extended leave of absence from the dental practice so that I could be with her every minute and provide the postoperative care she needed. I wasn't a medical doctor, but I was certainly capable of changing her dressings, measuring her fluids and administering her medications.

When Deborah first came home after the mastectomy, she was required to sleep upright for two weeks and not use her hands or move her upper body. She was limited to a lift chair and needed assistance with her basic needs; I helped her with these just as she had done for me after my accident.

Once she was able to recline again, some friends of ours thoughtfully brought a hospital bed to our house. I had assumed that Deborah would be most comfortable in the bed she was accustomed to, but the hospital bed with its many features was a definite advantage. She asked that we place it in the living room, instead of our bedroom, so that she could see what was happening and feel as if she was a part of everything we did. Of course, we complied. I continued to sleep on the living room couch so that I could stay next to her.

The next step of Deborah's treatment plan was to be chemotherapy, but when changing her dressing I noticed signs of possible infection at one of the surgical suture lines. I took a photograph, sent it to her plastic surgeon and he concurred.

For four weeks, Deborah had to have daily infusions of antibiotics, with each session lasting two hours. The chemotherapy couldn't begin until after this regimen was completed.

Once the infection was eliminated, her chemo treatments commenced and lasted until July. Next came a month of radiation from August to September, then reconstruction in October and implant surgery in December.

Throughout all those challenging, painful and frightening months, she never once complained. Among her greatest concerns was not her own well-being, but the effect that her illness might have on others. She worried especially about our grandchildren, since they were too young to understand why "Grandma Debbie" looked so unwell and wasn't able to play with them or take them for ice cream.

I always knew that my wife had many remarkable qualities. Seeing her fight all year long to beat her cancer revealed to me that among those qualities were a remarkable strength and an indomitable spirit.

***

I wasn't the only one impressed with Deborah's consistently positive attitude. Her oncologist was also struck by her determination and upbeat demeanor. She asked Deborah if she would mind speaking to another patient of hers who was having difficulty coping with the ordeal and had little support from family or friends.

Deborah has a huge heart and loves helping other people. She began speaking with the other patient on a regular basis, encouraging her through the treatment process.

Soon, word began to get around about Deborah, and she was sought out for counseling by other women at the oncology center. The conversations were typical by telephone, but she was able to meet with some of them in person. Sometimes, she explained the procedures and the sequence of treatment to them; Deborah had long experience describing treatment plans to patients through her work in my dental office, and she could do so clearly and in simple language. Most often, she simply provided the women with encouragement and emotional support.

As helpful as she was to the other cancer patients, I think her counseling activities also benefited Deborah. She was necessarily limited in what she could do physically, but she discovered that she was able to make a valuable contribution by speaking with other patients. It's always a morale boost to know that you've made a positive impact on someone else's life.

By the end of 2020, Deborah's treatment was complete and her prognosis positive. We were able to make plans to go on with our lives again, and knew that would cherish the coming years all the more from having gone through that experience.

19. The Third Act

I would be turning sixty-seven in 2022, and was contemplating what my life's third act would be like. Although we had fought our way through them successfully, the health scares of recent years made it frightening clear that that tomorrow is promised to no one. I wanted to live the rest of my life as fully as I could, and decided to retire from dentistry so that Deborah and I could spend our next years pursuing whatever interests most appealed to us.

In the spring of that year, we were all doing well. Deborah was going for regular checkups and there were no signs of the cancer recurring. I had started getting acupuncture treatment for my back pain; although I'd initially been skeptical about the technique, it did provide relief. Jessica was happily married with two children and expecting a third. Bryan, always interested in boats and sailing, lived at a marina on a boat of his own.

My parents, also healthy apart from the usual afflictions of old age, were still alive and living in New Jersey. I was banned from their house, but telephoned my mother every other day; those conversations were brief, usually no more than a couple of minutes, before my father would tell her to hang up. I had almost no contact with my brothers or sister, and we all preferred it that way.

As I thought of what retirement would be like, I realized that I would have no trouble keeping busy. A lot of projects and plans were already in the works.

Many of them involved film and television. I'd had several requests to appear in other reality shows, but had never wanted to commit to such a long stretch of production time again. Deborah, however, was just getting started as a television personality. She was among the cast of a different kind of reality program. Instead of a show that was all about drama, with bickering and backbiting, this new program focused on inspirational women making a positive impact in their communities. The pilot had been filmed and several episodes were in the works, with Deborah in a prominent role.

Among my upcoming media appearances was *Movie Money Confidential*. This was a documentary film on the financial end of movie production. It featured Burt Reynolds in his final film, as well as Salma Hayak, Scott duPont and—in a very small role—me. My participation in this movie was another happy result of my memorable Crystal Reel Awards presentation years earlier. In addition to being in the movie, I was asked to be a panelist in a discussion forum at the premiere—another chance for me to talk!

For years, I had been encouraged to produce a book of my photography. I'd had individual photos published, and a number of them appeared in an exhibit, but I hadn't had a chance to present a complete collection in book form. Now, I would have the time to take on such a project.

Deborah and I also discussed the trips we could take together once I retired. Alaska, which neither of us had ever visited, was at the top of our list. We also wanted to travel to Italy again, as well as Costa Rica and a few other countries.

Then, as I was mulling over all the possibilities for the future, I got the phone call that started me looking back on my life.

***

After that first conversation with my previously unknown half-sister Susan, the two of us spoke almost every day. Initially, much of our discussion was about the past. Susan had close ties to the Brooklyn neighborhood where I'd grown up—she even went to the same elementary school that I'd attended—and was a wealth of information. She knew things about families and neighbors that I had never imagined.

As the weeks went by, though, Susan and I spoke less of the past and more about our present lives. We became good friends over the phone and established an easy rapport. Deborah was delighted that I finally had a sibling with whom I could have a positive relationship. I no longer referred to Susan as my "half-sister." She was my "sister" and I was happy to have her as part of the family.

It became clear to Deborah, and Susan and I agreed, that there was something more we needed to do: We should meet in person.

20. A Fresh Start

Our chance came in August. Deborah's friend Connie from college, who still lived in New Jersey, had invited us to the wedding of her daughter. I would be driving us up there and we planned to stay for a couple of weeks.

Susan lives on Staten Island, so I suggested that we get together during that trip. She eagerly agreed and we decided to choose a time and place after the wedding.

We had known Connie since she and Deborah were education majors together at Fairleigh Dickinson, and were very close despite living so far apart. Prior to the wedding, we spent quite a bit of time with Connie and her family, catching up and helping with the arrangements.

The wedding itself was a beautiful affair in Woodcliff Lake, and Deborah and I were honored to be there. Once it was over and the newlyweds off to their honeymoon, we spent some additional time with Connie, everyone more relaxed now that the stress of planning a wedding was over.

Then, having enjoyed a few marvelous days with an old friend, it was time to meet a new one. I sought a location that would be convenient for both Susan and us. I looked at a map and noticed that Atlantic Highlands appeared to be a good choice. It was a place that was very special to me, since that was where Deborah and I had gotten engaged. In fact, the same restaurant was still there and that's where Susan and I planned to meet for lunch.

***

Deborah and I arrived early at Bahrs Landing, a quaint waterfront restaurant renowned for its fresh seafood. Bahrs Landing had been in business for more than a century, so it was little surprise that it looked almost the same as it had in 1978.

The restaurant wasn't yet open when we got to the door, but they let us in so that Deborah could use the restroom. While I waited, I looked around and spotted the table where we had sat when Deborah became my fiancée. I pointed it out to the manager, telling him, "I proposed to my wife at that table forty-four years ago."

He promised that we could have it again today.

Susan, wearing an attractive sundress, arrived with her husband Domenic and we all exchanged hugs. By now, my sister and I had seen each other's pictures on social media, so we recognized each other immediately. In person, I could see some physical resemblance to other women in our family. She had dark auburn hair, and her facial features reminded me of Sandra Bullock. Happily, the only Bilancione traits that Susan possessed were in her looks, not her personality, which was warm and friendly.

Domenic was a handsome, soft-spoken man who worked in computer technology. He didn't say much during lunch, which Susan later told me was unusual for him. But he felt that my sister and I should get to know each other as much as possible, so he thoughtfully let us do most of the talking.

There was no awkwardness during the meal, just a lot of conversation and laughter. It was like a family reunion, except it was between people meeting for the first time. Over clam chowder and lobster rolls, we talked about our present lives, especially our children and grandchildren. Susan and Domenic had two sons and I looked forward to meeting my nephews someday.

We didn't discuss any of the unpleasant aspects of our histories and there were no new revelations. My sister and I had already covered those in our phone conversations.

Susan did comment at one point, "I can't get over how normal and nice you are! You're so different from the other Bilancione men." She hesitated before asking, "What do you think it was that made them the way they are?"

"My father and uncles got a lot of it from their father," I replied. "He was a nasty, violent man. That's what they knew, and that's how they grew up."

There was another factor, too, which I didn't mention. Part of the reason our family dynamics were so difficult was that there were too many families involved in it. Even my father and my late Uncle Sal, who had been so close growing up, were at odds later in life. Uncle Sal told his children to avoid my father because he ran around with "the wrong kind of people." The issue wasn't that my father was involved with criminals, but that they were the wrong criminals. Uncle Sal lived and worked in Gambino territory, while my father operated with the Genovese. Conflicts between those two families sometimes caused rifts in ours.

Lunch went on for two hours and the conversation never stalled. When we finally had to go, we agreed to get together again. The next time, they would come down to Florida and we would show them around Orlando and take them to the beaches.

Although the main reason for the lunch was for Susan and I to meet, sitting at the same table where I had proposed to Deborah also had me thinking back to that evening so long ago. Just before we got up to leave, I looked at my wife and we exchanged smiles. And I saw that she remains every bit as beautiful as when she agreed to marry me.

**

On the long drive back to Florida, with Deborah sleeping on the seat next to me, I reflected on the meeting with my sister. Somehow, I felt rejuvenated. Earlier in the year, I had been thinking of retirement and how some aspects of my life were winding down. Now I realized that there was still a lot ahead.

Although Susan's initial phone call had been something of a shock, and triggered some unpleasant memories, the end result of her reaching out to me was entirely positive. I had a wonderful new person in my life whom I was proud to call "family."

In fact, it was emotionally invigorating to discover that there were still surprises like that in store for me. I knew that there would be more of them in the future, and I could look forward to meeting new people, traveling to unfamiliar places and embarking on fresh adventures.

No doubt there would more challenges ahead, too. But when they came, I would face them the same way that I had throughout my life: I would rise to meet them.

Acknowledgements

The authors are very grateful to our families, friends and colleagues who encouraged and assisted us throughout the writing of this book. Special thanks go to Deborah Bilancione, Jennifer Soos, Connie Stack, Alison Johnson and Meredith Bernstein.

About the Authors

Carl Bilancione is best known to national television audiences as Dr. Carl from *Survivor Africa*. A graduate of Fairleigh Dickinson and a U. S. Navy veteran, he established a successful dental practice in Winter Park, Florida. He delights in challenging himself and has completed the New York, London and Marine Corps marathons. Carl is an accomplished photographer, specializing in wildlife and sports photography. Always seeking to help and inspire others, he is active in charitable organizations such as Hearts of Reality and Give Kids the World Village. In addition to *Survivor Africa*, his television and radio appearances include *Live with Regis and Kelly*, *The Late Late Show with Craig Kilborn*, and the *Howard Stern Show*. He has hosted several sports talk shows on television and radio.

***

Troy Soos is the author of twelve books, including the best-selling Mickey Rawlings mystery series. His work has been praised by the *New York Times*, *USA Today*, *Sports Illustrated* and *Publishers Weekly*. He has been a guest on National Public Radio and Voice of America.